AMERICAN RAILROAD STOCK CERTIFICATES

AMERICAN RAILROAD STOCK CERTIFICATES

Anne-Marie Hendy

Stanley Gibbons Publications Ltd
391 Strand, London WC2R 0LX

By appointment to Her Majesty The Queen
Stanley Gibbons Ltd, London
Philatelists

© Stanley Gibbons Publications Ltd 1980
First Published 1980
ISBN 0 85259 296 5

Printed by
Bemrose Specialist Print, Derby

CONTENTS

Preface	vii
Introduction	1
History of the early railroad companies	1
The American Banknote Co.	3
Note on State and Municipal bonds	6
Bibliography	7
American Railroads and their Stock Certificates	9
Price Guide to the Certificates	161
Appendix: Biographies of Cornelius Vanderbilt and Jay Gould	165

Colour Plates between pages 88 and 89.

PREFACE

Until recently there has been relatively little interest in bonds and share certificates whether or not they related to railway companies.

The last few years has seen an unexpectedly large growth of interest in all things collectable and relics of the great age of railways have shared in this growth.

Railroad certificates appeal to a variety of students and collectors—those interested in industrial history; in the development of financial institutions; in design and typography as well as to the ubiquitous railway enthusiast.

The following notes on collecting will, it is hoped, be of help to those new to this field and are based on the experience gained by the author and her husband in building up their collection.

Collectors' bond and share certificates are either in issued or unissued form. Unissued certificates, which are blank, lacking the company's seal, date, stockholder's name (in the case of registered stock) and in many cases the signatures of the company officials, never possessed any investment value. They were held in reserve by the company to be issued as and when required to future investors. When two identical certificates occur, but one is issued whereas the other is not, collectors usually prefer the issued one, although because of this very fact it can show signs of wear while the unissued document can be expected to be in pristine condition.

However, in certain cases, unissued certificates can command high values, generally when no issued examples are known to exist. In the developing years of American railways, when thousands of new companies were formed, some on less than sound foundations, it could happen that a newly incoporated company was either liquidated due to the lack of funds or taken over before it had time to issue its shares.

As in other collecting fields, condition plays an important part in determining the value of historical bond and share certificates. Because they were traded instruments, passing from hand to hand, issued certificates cannot be expected to occur in mint condition. But there is a wide margin of difference between a certificate in very fine condition with only minimal signs of wear, and a ragged and tatty one whose value becomes correspondingly diminished.

Sometimes, a certificate in poor condition may become quite acceptable to collectors, if only a handful of examples of a particular issue are known to remain in existence and all of these have turned up in a much used or even damaged state. Certificates which ceased to be valid on the stock exchange were cancelled, either by punch-holes or by cuts through the documents. Random punch-hole cancellations have often spoilt decorative vignettes or famous signatures on a certificate and collectors are advised to look out for less mutilated examples.

In general, most items are found with one or two folds. After acquiring an old bond or share certificate, the collector should make sure that his document is stored flat and unfolded. The easiest and most practical way to keep a collection is to house it in ring-albums which display one certificate (or more, depending on size) on each page and can accommodate new insertions without disturbing the order.

Finally, a collection should not only be properly and neatly housed, it should also be written up. Any relevant information on a particular item, whether it concerns the fate of the company or the men who signed the certificate, etc., ought to be recorded alongside when it is known, as even the best memory is liable to fail and forget interesting facts after a number of years.

Leatherhead, Surrey   ANNE-MARIE HENDY

INTRODUCTION

History of the early railway companies

Since the formation in 1827 of the first public railway company, roughly nine thousand different railway companies have been incorporated in the United States. With the numerous changes in capital structure, reorganisations, takeovers and mergers which have taken place over more than one century of railway history, this can be only an approximate figure as, at given times, the total number of companies either increased or contracted. For the collector of old bonds and shares it means that building a complete collection of American railway bonds and share certificates practically amounts to a physical impossibility.

The purpose of this book is simply to group by alphabetical order of companies some 150 of the most attractive and interesting among American railway certificates, irrespective of their value or scarcity. The earliest certificate illustrated originates from 1836 (New York, Providence and Boston Railroad Co.) while the most recent is a certificate dated 1975 of the now liquidated Penn Central Co.

More than any other industry, the development of railways contributed much to opening up the vast territory of the United States and transforming the country in less than a hundred years into one of the world's leading economic powers. Throughout the nineteenth century and well into the twentieth, the iron rail held a dominant place in the world of communications until it was gradually superseded by the automobile and the aeroplane in terms of socio-economic importance.

Towards the end of the eighteenth century before the introduction of the railway in the United States, early settlers concentrated mainly along the coast and the big waterways. The Alleghany Mountains marked the natural barrier between the eastern states and the isolated territories to the west. Recognizing the economic potential for the country if the communications system were developed, George Washington, alluding to the vast regions in the west, said prophetically: ". . . but smooth the road and make easy the way for them, and then see what an influx of articles will be poured upon us, how amazingly our exports will increase, and how amply we shall be compensated for any trouble and expense we may encounter to effect it". Despite his strong recommendations for the building of canals, at that time the great transport innovation, no great work of the kind was undertaken, mainly because of the lack of adequate means. Eventually, as the cost of moving goods slowly on the old highways kept rising with corresponding high deployment of labour, pressure to improve the system of communications resulted in a charter granted in 1817 to build the Erie canal, opened in 1825. Connecting Albany on the Hudson river, to Buffalo on Lake Erie, the canal not only enabled goods from the interior of the country to find a ready outlet at the harbout of New York but also to be transported much cheaper and faster than by the traditional methods. Freight rates dropped from $100 to $20 per ton and the journey was effected in eight days rather than twenty. Within fifteen years of the completion of the Erie canal, no less than 8500 miles of canals were built in the United States, both by public and private corporations, but very few proved profitable. This was due to the inherent limitations of canal navigation and to the strong competition of a new challenger, the railway.

The first public railway in the United States, the Baltimore & Ohio Railroad, was chartered in 1827 by merchants of the city of Baltimore in order to improve the trade they received from the west. Since the opening of the Erie canal, this had been largely diverted to New York instead. As a canal from Baltimore to the Ohio river proved impractical because of the intervening mountain range, the choice fell on the construction of a railway which was officially started on 4 July 1828 by Charles Carroll, the only surviving signatory of the Declaration of Independence, who said after the ceremony of inauguration: "I consider this among the most important acts of my life, second only to that of signing the Declaration of Independence, if even second to that". The first fifteen mile section of the Baltimore & Ohio Railroad opened in 1830, with horses providing the driving power. But already in 1831 steam traction was adopted. No sooner did railways demonstrate their superiority over all other contemporary transport methods than countless schemes were projected. Many of the early railways were built following the course of a river or canal, or linking two major rivers or canal systems. Individual states and municipal bodies contributed to a large extent to the construction of new railways, sometimes assisting or controlling major projects, as they had done earlier with canals. Railway lines were built from a mine head to the nearest river port, or from industrial or agricultural centres to major ports, emphasizing the early dependence of rail transport on navigation.

After the Baltimore & Ohio Railroad, the next important railway to be constructed was the South Carolina Railroad, first opened for traffic in 1833. With its 135 miles, it was the longest railway in the world at that time. In the pioneering years, new railway lines were built mainly in the industrial states on the east cost. The next step to be undertaken was to extend the northern railway system to Chicago. Then the great trunk lines based on Boston, New York, Philadelphia and Baltimore progressed westward to the middle states. The Chicago & Rock Island Railroad, completed in 1854, became the first line to reach the Mississipi from Chicago. From then onwards, much of the trade was directed to Chicago instead of down river to New Orleans which suffered accordingly.

The railway systems in the North, of which the Baltimore & Ohio is the most southern, progressed much more vigorously than in the South because the North had far greater capital resources and was supported by communities of greater economic strength. South of Baltimore, there was no major commercial city on the Atlantic coast. New Orleans, though a major port, lost an increasing proportion of the trade with the interior which sought outlets to large eastern cities in order to reach a market in Europe. In striking contrast to the railway development in the North, the southern states showed a smaller railway milage in proportion to the size of their territories and smaller revenues. Southern railways were in fact tributaries to the big northern systems.

From the 1860s a great thrust forward was made to extend the railway to the west of the Missouri river. Stretching into Indian territory (like the Missouri, Kansas & Texas Railroad) as far as Colorado (such as the Kansas Pacific Railroad), these new railways crossed very sparsely populated regions, greatly helping to develop trade by opening up vast new territories and new markets. Construction work progressed at a forced pace, achieving as much as one mile per day in the case of the Union Pacific and the Central Pacific, the only railways sponsored by the federal government, which reached the Californian coast over the Rocky Mountains. The first train bound for San Francisco left New York on 1 July 1876, arriving at its destination after 83 hours 53 minutes' running time. Except for the construction of the Pacific railroads and their branches, railway development proceeded otherwise without reference to any general plan or supervision from the states. With each year, freight could be transported further and yet transport rates were considerably reduced.

In the latter half of the nineteenth century the Pacific states represented the growth area for railways, whereas in other states they suffered a depression in their earnings. During the twentieth century the number of railway companies continued to fall, in a steady trend which aimed towards centralisation of the various systems and resulted from the development of alternative methods of transport gradually superseding the long hegemony of the rail.

The bonds and share certificates issued by countless railway companies reflect the history of the development of the industry. New loans hastily arranged in quick succession are testimonies of the initial difficulties in constructing and financing the railway; the distribution of fat dividends indicate periods of success and prosperity, while complicated stock market transactions on a vast scale often reveal the bitter struggle for control between rival companies.

During the period of consolidation and expansion of American railways, a whole generation of railway magnates founded or increased their wealth entirely through railway speculation—men like Cornelius Vanderbilt, his son William, Jay Gould the railway financier and stock market operator, ex-stockbroker Edward Harriman and his rival James Hill who, among others, rose to fame and riches in the second half of the nineteenth century. Far from pioneering in a new and original field, and thereby risking their capital in untried ventures, they took advantage of whatever opportunities presented themselves at a time when the railway had long become an accepted and established means of transport offering rich promises for expansion. Through clever stock manipulations which enabled them to acquire company after company in takeovers and mergers, these giants of railway finance controlled vast empires representing thousands of miles of track, concentrated in a single unit to which new lines were added, mostly built in the vast tracts of virgin land to the west.

The American Banknote Co.
Because of the leading role played by the American Banknote Co. in designing and printing not only banknotes but also bonds and share certificates of all kinds, it seems appropriate to give a brief outline of the development of this company. As bonds and shares can represent very large values, much in excess of the actual cost of the paper and the printing, it became essential for firms producing the certificates to ensure that first, they could not be easily counterfeited and second, that the plates used would be kept under

strict control so that they would not become available to others. At the same time, the certificates had to reflect the importance and distinction of the issuing company and of the value they represented.

Dating back to Paul Revere, the engraver of independent America's first banknotes, the industry of security printing developed rapidly in the United States thanks to the inventions and improvements introduced by several talented men. Jacob Perkins began the widespread use of strengthened steel plates for engraving, while Asa Spencer developed engravings produced with the geometric lathe. This creates swirls too complex and too precise to be copied freehand or reproduced by machine if its correct setting is not known. Designs obtained by the geometric lathe often decorate the borders of share certificates. Combining advanced techniques and high artistic quality, the early firms of engraving contributed to making counterfeiting an increasingly difficult task.

In 1818 the firm of Murray, Draper, Fairman & Co., an early forerunner of the American Banknote Co., made a number of recommendations to the Bank of England regarding the methods of banknote printing. Perfection in design, steel engraving and the adoption of figured borders of great variety, evenness and accuracy that can only be obtained by machine, figured among the points stressed. Just before the formation of the American Banknote Co., the dominant firm in the industry was Rawdon, Wright, Hatch and Edson, which began in 1828 when Ralph Rawdon opened an engraving firm in New York. After manufacturing stamps for a private messenger firm in New York, the company in 1847—the year a new partner, Tracy Edson, joined the company—secured the contract to produce the first postage stamps for the federal government. Edson's contribution was to expand the company by opening several offices throughout the country, in New Orleans, Cincinnati, Boston and Philadelphia. The use of the green colour on American banknotes is a tradition also associated with Rawdon, Wright, Hatch & Edson. The firm's Montreal partner had advocated printing banknotes in two colours, one of them green, to deter forgery by photography as the cameras of that time were unable to separate different colours. Another contemporary firm, Jocelyn, Draper, Welsh & Co., used reddish-brown as their second colour but the green survived.

On 28 April 1858, seven leading printing and engraving firms decided to merge into one institution, the American Banknote Co. It was not an original name as Jocelyn, Draper, Welsh & Co. employed it as early as 1854 in addition to their title. The seven who participated in the merger were each allocated a number of shares in the new company, which varied according to their relative importance. Of the seven firms, four had grown out of the partnership originally formed by Murray, Draper, Fairman & Co. in 1810. These were Danforth, Perkins & Co. (the firm which employed Asa Spencer), Bald Cousland & Co., Toppan Carpenter & Co. and finally Jocelyn, Draper, Welsh & Co. The three others were Rawdon, Wright, Hatch & Edson; Wellstood, Hay & Whiting; and John E. Gavit. In the autumn of 1859, those partners of Danforth, Wright & Co. who had not joined the American Banknote Co. as Danforth, Perkins & Co., formed the National Banknote Co. Twenty years later it was consolidated with its prototype.

Other than banknotes, printing bonds and share certificates represented another major business of the American Banknote Co. The artist Asher Durand, who started business with his brother Cyrus, an engraver, in New York in 1824, is responsible for the introduction of mythological figures, drawn in the Greek manner which gave their distinctive style to the vignettes on the bonds and share certificates engraved by the American Banknote Co. In later years, until his death in 1948, Alonzo E. Foringer continued the tradition of portaying Greek gods and goddesses. Many of his allegorical figures grace the vignettes on certificates issued during that period.

With the protection of the investing community in mind, the New York Stock Exchange published in 1874 new rules and recommendations applying to listed bonds and share certificates:

Committee on Securities
New York Stock Exchange

City of New York, Nov. 1874.

The numerous frauds practiced upon the community, in the Counterfeiting of Certificates of Stocks and Bonds, and the altering of Certificates from smaller to larger denominations, have compelled the Stock Exchange to use all precautions in their power against them, and to require in all future applications to place Securities on the List, that they shall be carefully engraved by some responsible Bank Note Engraving Company. They recommend that Certificates of Stock of One-hundred Shares should have the denomination conspicuously engraved thereon, and that Certificates of lesser denominations should be of a different style and color. Many Companies have already adopted this plan, and any that are still using a printed or lithographed Certificate, are requested, for their own protection as well as that of the public, to cease doing so, and to change to an engraved one at their earliest convenience.

Very respectfully,
Edward Brandon, Chairman.

Following an act of Congress passed in 1877 providing that all United States banknotes and securities be printed by the Federal Bureau of Engraving and Printing, the three companies that had formerly been entrusted with that work decided to consolidate. The merger of the National Bank Note Co. and the Continental Bank Note Co. with the American Banknote Co. took place on 27 December 1878. During the 1880s, the New York Stock Exchange issued new rulings concerning the standard of execution of certificates. In particular, it required that specimens be filed with the Stock Exchange (1885), that the work be done by an approved company, using two plates (one for black printing and one for colour) and that signatures be handwritten (1887). In 1890 it ruled that the text must be engraved by hand and that odd-lot certificates must carry punch-panels to prevent altering the number of shares written or typed on the certificate. Because of these strict requirements with which it was able to comply easily, the American Banknote Co. was occasionally accused by rival firms finding it hard to compete, of working in league with the Stock Exchange.

Other firms such as Western Bank Note Co., International Bank Note Co., Franklin-Lee Bank Note Co. and the British printer Bradbury, Wilkinson & Co. Ltd. later also became affiliated to the American Banknote Co.

Note on State and Municipal Bonds

At first, the construction of American railways proceeded without any plans or supervision from the states in which the railway companies were incorporated, except the Pacific railways which were chartered by the federal government in 1861. Acts of incorporation were granted as a matter of course. The state of New York was the first to pass a general railroad law in 1850, the effect of which was to override local and sectional legislation and to ensure that the railway system would meet the needs of the community.

During the period of fast railway development, individual states, counties or municipalities participated actively in financing certain railways in which they had a particular interest and wanted to see built. One way of helping a railway company was to make cheap land grants, especially in the vast and sparsely populated mid-western states. Another method was for a state, county or municipality to underwrite large blocks of a particular railway stock. In turn, the authorities would pay the company for their stockholdings from the proceeds of special railway construction bonds which they issued to the general public. Among the certificates illustrated there are a number of such state or municipal bonds.

BIBLIOGRAPHY

Reference books
Financial Stock Guide Service: **Directory of Obsolete Securities,** 1978–1979
Robert D. Fisher: **Manual of Valuable and Worthless Securities** (several volumes, New York, 1942–1975)
Robert D. Fisher: **Manual of Valuable Securities** (New York, 1943)
Oliver C. Klinger: **Obsolete Securities** (New York, 1923)
Moody's Transportation Manual (1977 edition)
H. V. Poor: **Manual of the Railroads of the United States** (New York, 1876–1898)
Marvyn Scudder: **Manual of Extinct or Obsolete Companies** (several volumes, New York, 1925–1940)
R. M. Smythe: **Valuable Extinct Securities** (New York, 1929)

General literature
F. L. Allen: **The Great Pierpoint Morgan** (London, 1949)
C. F. Carter: **When Railroads were new** (New York, 1926)
Henry Clews: **Twenty-five years in Wall Street** (New York, 1888)
C. J. Corliss: **Main Line of Mid-America** (New York, 1950)
J. F. Flynn: **Men of Wealth** (New York, 1941)
J. F. Gairns: **Railways for all** (3rd edition, London & Melbourne, 1929)
Julius Grodinsky: **Jay Gould: His Business Career, 1867–1892** (Philadelphia, 1957)
Agnes C. Laut: **The Romance of the Rails** (New York, 1936)
Meade Minnigerode: **Certain Rich Men** (New York, 1927)
J. G. Pangborn: **The World's Railway** (New York, 1894)
Frank H. Spearman: **The Strategy of Great Railroads** (New York, 1905)
Robert I. Warshow: **The Story of Wall Street** (New York, 1929)
C. Winchester (ed.): **Railway Wonders of the World** (2 vols., London, 1935)

AMERICAN RAILROADS AND THEIR STOCK CERTIFICATES

The Arkansas Midland Railroad Co.

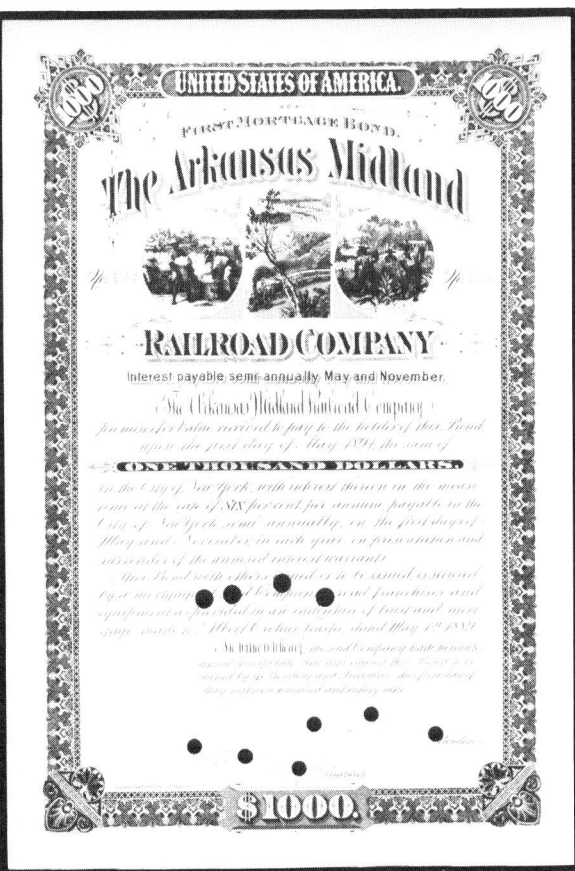

Six per cent five year first mortgage bond to bearer for $1000, issued on 1 May 1889 by The Arkansas Midland Railroad Co. The bond was secured by a mortgage on the company's railway, franchises and equipment. The certificate, bears the signature of the President at that time, A.H. Johnson.

Chartered under the name of Arkansas Central in 1853, the company opened the first fifty miles of line in 1871 but already in 1877 it had to be sold under foreclosure, although the company had received financial help from the state of Arkansas to the extent of $15,000 per mile for the construction of the railway. The bond illustrated here was issued by the new company organised on 15 May 1878 under the name of Arkansas Midland.

Atlantic City & Shore Railroad Co.

Registered certificate for five shares of $100 each in the capital stock of the Atlantic City & Shore Railroad Co., dated 16 April 1906. The picturesque vignettes, which enliven the certificate, could themselves pass as an advertisement for the town's attraction as a pleasant and bracing seaside resort, with its large hotels located right on the waterfront and its long sandy beaches.

Attica and Buffalo Rail Road Co.

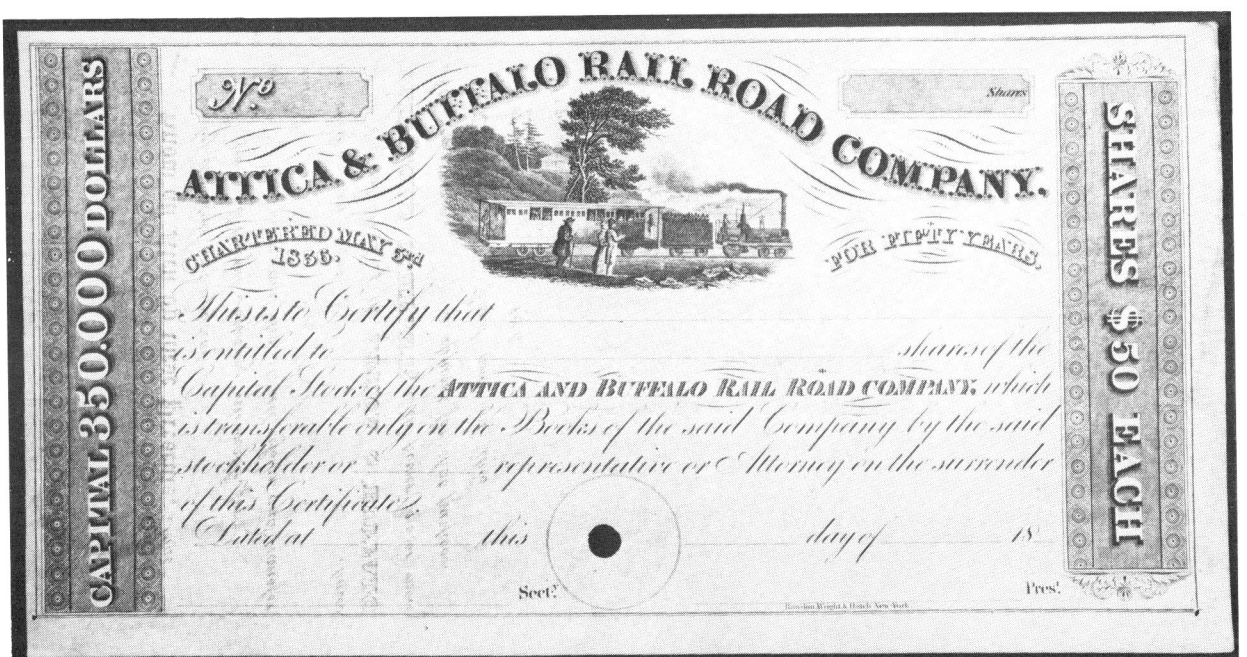

Unissued share certificate of the Attica and Buffalo Rail Road Co., chartered 'for fifty years' on 3 May 1836 with a share capital of $350,000. The railway was opened in 1842. The certificate reproduced here dates prior to 1842 as during that year the company was consolidated as the Buffalo and Rochester Railroad.

Baltimore and Ohio Rail Road Co.

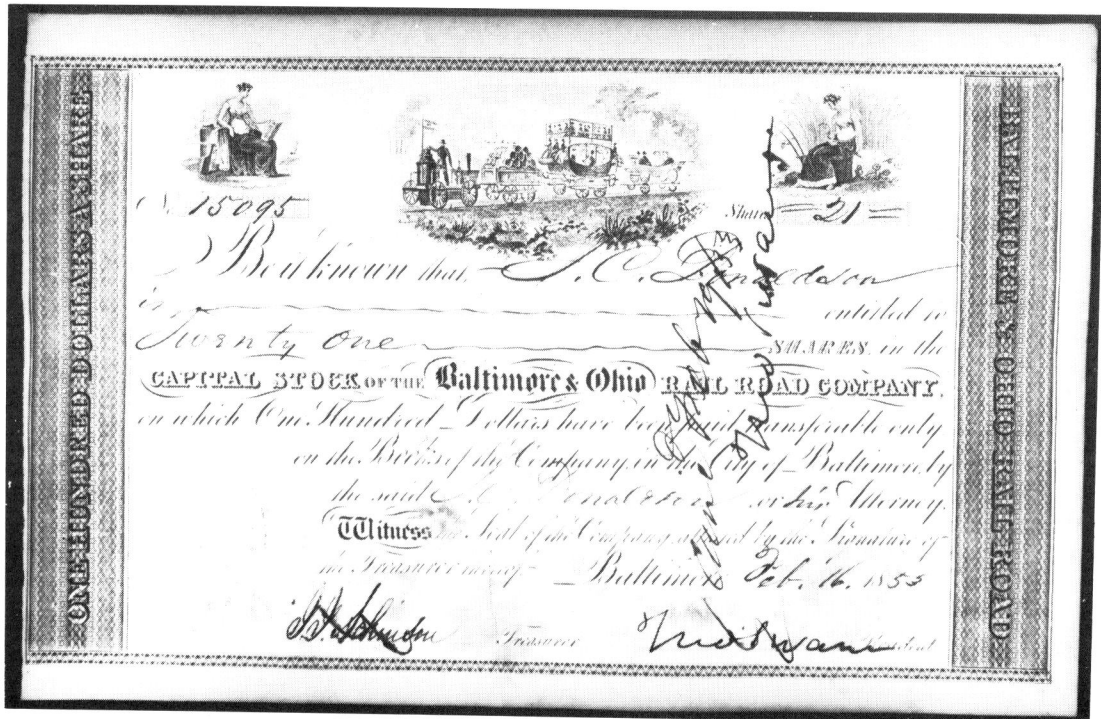

Registered certificate for 21 shares of $100 each in the capital stock of the Baltimore and Ohio Railroad Co., dated 16 February 1853.

Chartered in 1827 by Baltimore merchants in a bid to restore to their city much of the trade from the West which had been diverted to the recently constructed Erie Canal, the company started in 1828 the construction of the railway, the first passenger railway in the country. The first section of fifteen miles opened in 1830. The company made history again by becoming the first railway to use American locomotives, starting with Peter Cooper's *Tom Thumb*, a small experimental engine with vertical boiler and cylinders. But Phineas Davis's *York*, which won its constructor a prize of $4000 in 1831, was the wholly American-built steam engine chosen by the company after a contest and put into regular service on the line. The certificate illustrated here bears the signature of President Thomas Swann who, after managing to dispose of $1 million worth of previously unsaleable bonds to Baring Brothers, the London merchant bankers in 1848 obtained the necessary funds to complete the construction of the railway to the Ohio River.

Baltimore and Ohio Railroad Co.

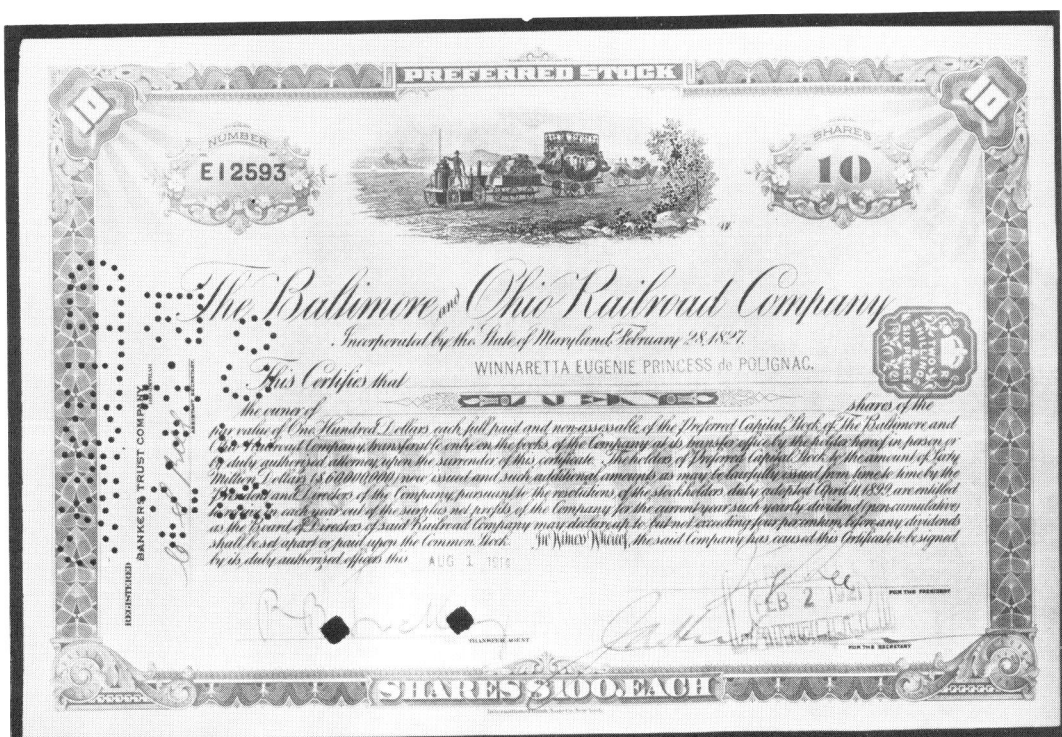

This later certificate for 10 shares, dated 1 August 1914, was registered in Britain in the name of Winnaretta Eugenie Princess de Polignac, a member of an old French aristocratic family, and bears a British embossed revenue stamp for 2s. 6d. Like the preceding example, the romantic engraving showing the little *Tom Thumb* pulling a number of passenger coaches was chosen to grace the vignette on the certificate.

Baltimore and Ohio Southwestern Railway Co.

Certificate for 10 shares of $100 each registered in the name of Henry Oppenheimer, London, and dated 27 January 1899. The same vignette depicting a steam train and station also appears on the certificates of the Cincinnati, Washington and Baltimore Railroad Co.

The Baltimore and Ohio Southwestern Railway Co. emerged in 1893 as a reorganisation of the Baltimore and Ohio Southwestern Railroad Co. (whose share certificates look identical to the present one except for the slight name change) and the Ohio and Mississippi Railway Co. In 1899 it was sold under foreclosure by the Farmers Loan and Trust Co.

Boston Consolidated Street Railway Co.

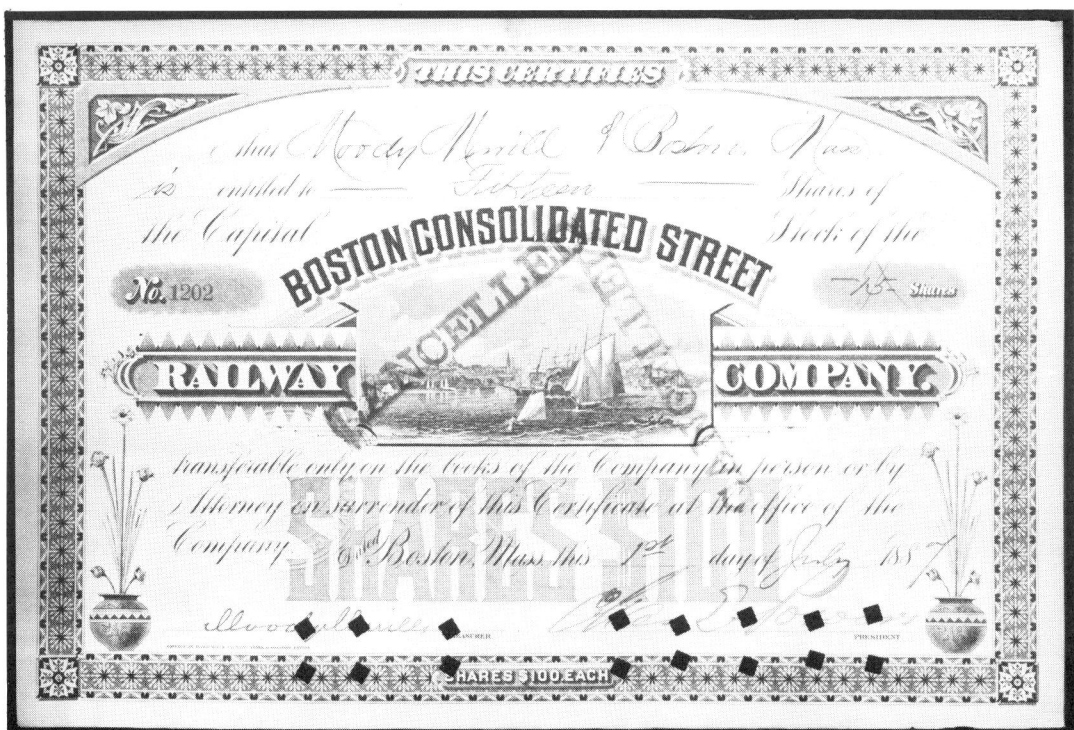

Registered certificate for 15 shares in the Boston Consolidated Street Railway Co. dated 1 July 1887. Before the invention of electricity, city tramways were operated with horse-drawn vehicles. The attractive vignette shows a busy harbour scene, with a number of sailing vessels plying the water, and the city skyline outlined in the background.

Boston, Hartford and Erie Railroad Co.

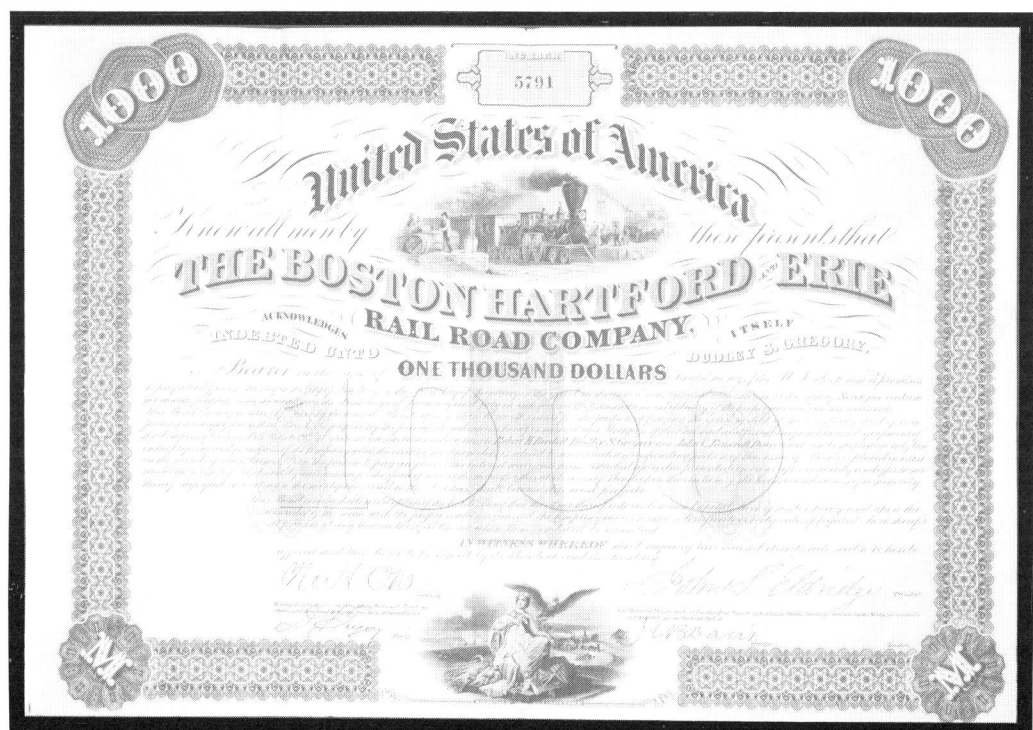

Seven per cent mortgage bond to bearer for $1000 issued by the Boston, Hartford and Erie Railroad Co. on 19 March 1866. The certificate was engraved by the National Banknote Co., New York.

The company had been chartered in 1863 as successor to various incomplete railways. Named after one of the mortgage trustees, these 'Berdell' bonds, of which 20,000 were issued to a total of $20 million, represented the cost of the railway. In 1873 the company was reorganised as the New York and New England Railroad Co. This certificate is signed by John S. Eldridge, the company's forceful president who, during the 1860s, joined forces with Jay Gould against Cornelius Vanderbilt in a bid to obtain control of the Erie Railroad.

(This certificate is illustrated in colour—Plate 1.)

Boston and New York Air Line Railroad Co.

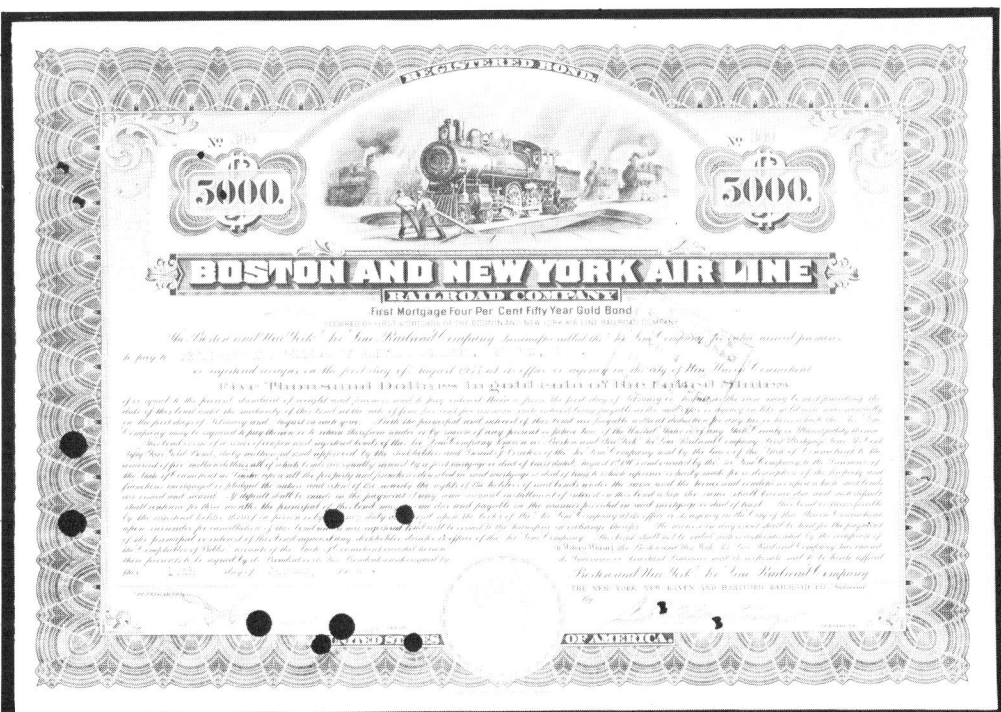

First mortgage four per cent 50 year gold bond for $5000, issued in August 1905 by the Boston and New York Air Line Railroad Co. and registered in the name of the President and Fellows of Harvard College, Boston, Mass. The certificate is dated 10 January 1925 after the company was taken over in 1907 by the New York, New Haven and Hartford Railroad Co., which had been leasing the Boston and New York Air Line Railroad since 1883. The original charter had been granted to the New York & Boston Railroad Co. in 1846. The present title was adopted at the time of the company's reorganisation in 1875. The term *Air Line*, sometimes used by railway companies, was intended to convey the idea that the railway took the fastest and most direct route between two cities.

Boston and Providence Railroad Corporation

Registered certificate for six shares of the Boston and Providence Railroad Corporation, dated 27 June 1871.

One of the earliest railway companies in the United States, it was chartered in the state of Massachusetts in June 1831. The line opened to Providence, Rhode Island, a distance of 44 miles, in 1835. For the year 1871–1872, the company paid 10 per cent dividends.

The Canon City and Cripple Creek (State of Colorado) Electric Railway Co.

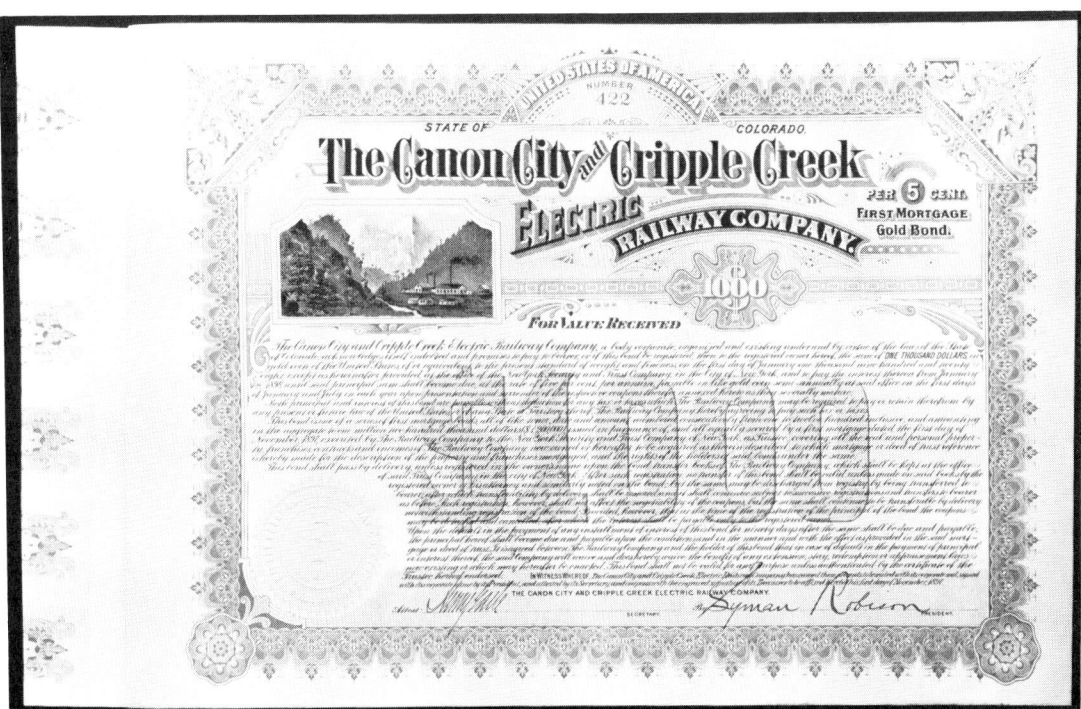

Five per cent first mortgage gold bond to bearer for $1000, issued on 1 November 1897 by The Canon City and Cripple Creek Electric Railway Co. The bonds matured after 30 years with both the principal and interest payable free of taxes. The total issue amounted to $1,200,000, divided into $1000 bonds, and was secured by a mortgage on the railway's property and equipment.

Canton, Aberdeen and Nashville Rail Road Co. (State of Mississippi)

First mortgage twenty-five year gold bond to bearer for $1000 issued by the Canton, Aberdeen and Nashville Railroad Co. on 1 December 1884. The total issue amounted to $2 million, divided into 2000 bonds of $1000 each.

The railway company, incorporated in Mississippi in February 1882, was owned and operated by the Illinois Central Railroad Co. which had appointed their General Manager, James C. Clarke, President of the new company after he had advocated the construction of feeder lines from the undeveloped but potentially rich cotton-producing region of the Mississippi delta. The line opened for operation in August 1884. One of the trustees for the mortgage was Stuyvesant Fish, a railway financier, himself associated with the Illinois Central and son of Hamilton Fish, Secretary of State under President Grant. Both Fish and Clarke later became Presidents of the Illinois Central Railroad.

Chicago, Burlington and Quincy Railroad Co.

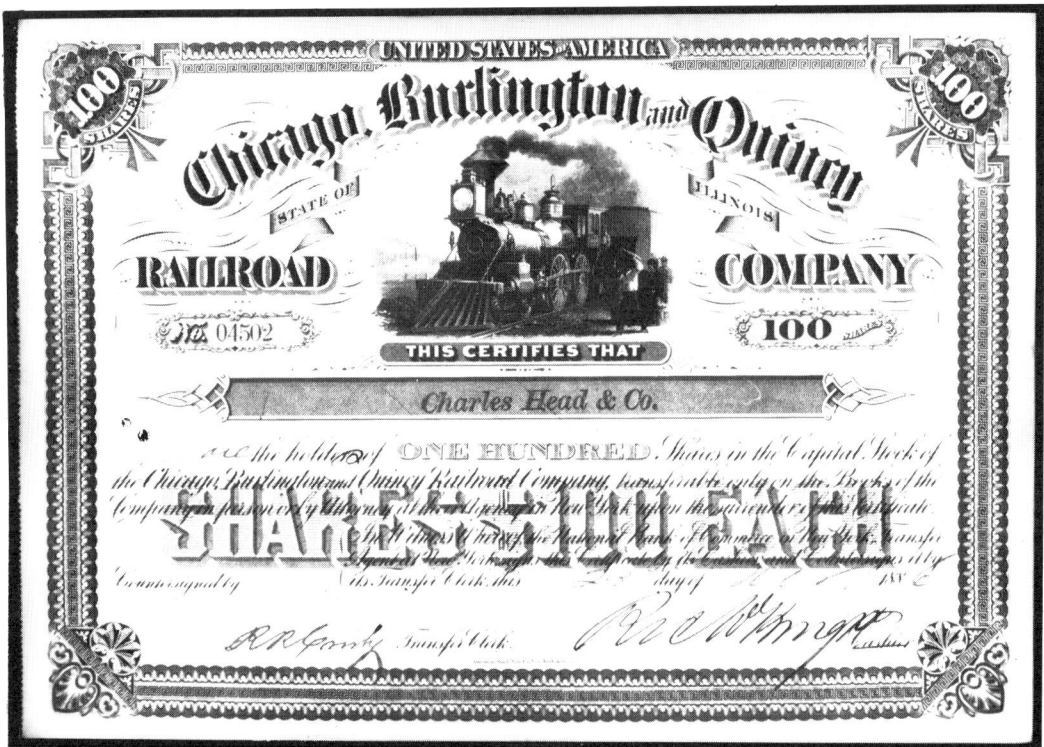

Registered certificate for 100 shares in the capital stock of the Chicago, Burlington and Quincy Railroad Co., dated 23 November 1886.

The first section of this railway, which by 1886 operated a large network over six states totalling over 3000 miles of track, was built from Chicago to Mendota by the Chicago and Aurora Railroad Co., under a charter granted in 1852. In 1855 the name of that company was changed to the Chicago, Burlington and Quincy Railroad Co. In 1868 the company began the construction of a number of lines which were leased, but were effectively owned by and incorporated into the Chicago, Burlington and Quincy system. In 1886, the President of the company was Charles E. Perkins who, in his drive for expansion, clashed on several occasions with Jay Gould over the control and acquisition of rival lines. Much later, James Hill together with J. P. Morgan, acquired a majority shareholding in 1901 and the company passed into the Hill railway system.

Chicago and Eastern Illinois Railroad Co.

Unissued certificate of the 1880s for 100 shares in the capital stock of the Chicago and Eastern Illinois Railroad Co., which succeeded the Chicago, Danville and Vincennes Railroad Co. after the latter was sold under foreclosure in 1877. The vignette shows an engraving of the steam train named "Progress".

The company operated a short line, 250 miles in length, of which part was leased from other companies.

Chicago and Eastern Illinois Railroad Co.

Registered certificate for 50 shares of $100 each in the preferred stock of the Chicago and Eastern Illinois Railroad Co., dated 8 March 1898. The counterfoil of the certificate, of a design different from that of the preceding one, mentions the price paid by the shareholder, $3088·50.

Chicago Great Western Railroad Co.

This fairly recent certificate for 10 shares of $100 each in the Chicago Great Western Railroad Co., incorporated in the state of Illinois, was registered in Great Britain and bears a two-shilling British revenue stamp. It is dated 7 April 1937.

The company was reorganised as the Chicago, Great Western Railway Co. (Illinois) on 19 February 1941. Shareholders of the common stock received no equity in the new company, but holders of preferred shares could exchange theirs on the basis of two for one new common share. On 31 December 1955, the Chicago, Great Western Railway Co. (Ill.) was re-incorporated under the laws of Delaware. It merged into the Chicago & Northwestern Railway Co. in 1968.

Chicago, Lake Geneva and Pacific Railway Co.

Unissued registered share certificate in the Chicago, Lake Geneva and Pacific Railway Co., which was incorporated in the state of Wisconsin with a share capital of $2 million, divided into 20,000 shares of $100 each. The detailed vignette of a group of country folk waving at a passing train shows that the company had laid a double track and installed a telegraph along the line.

Chicago and Northwestern Railway Co.

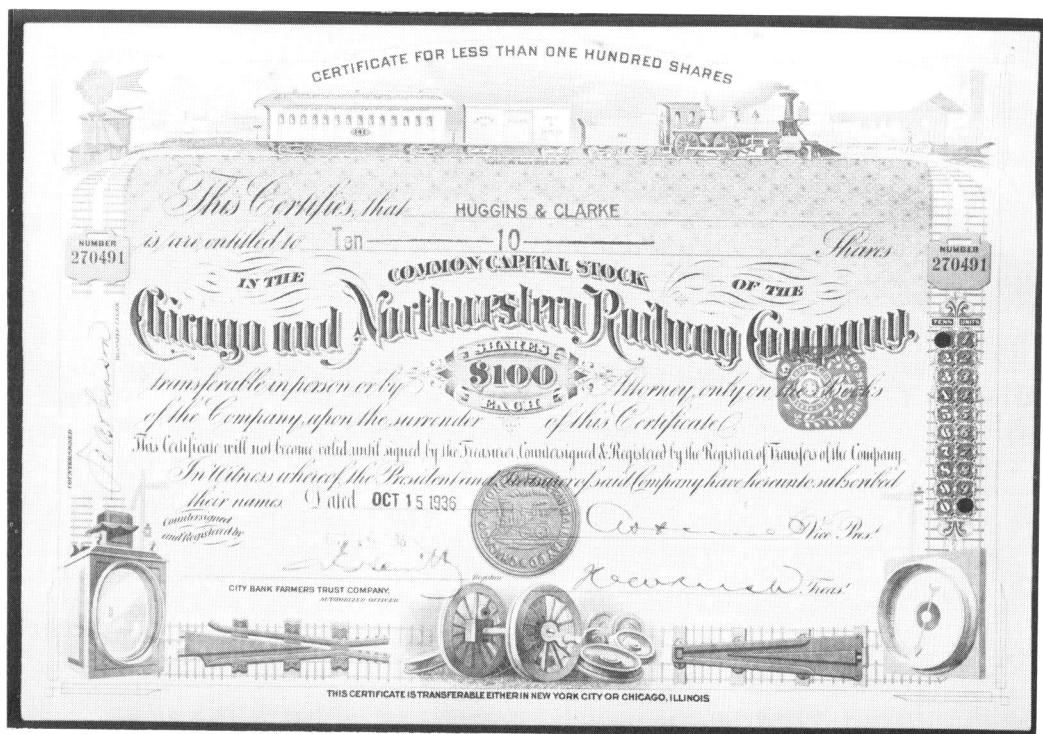

Registered certificate for 10 shares of $100 each in the common capital stock of the Chicago and Northwestern Railway Co., dated 15 October 1936 and bearing a British two-shilling embossed revenue stamp.

The original railway company was organised in 1859 as successor to the Chicago, St. Paul and Fond du Lac Railroad Co. At that time, its completed mileage totalled 176 miles. By the mid-1880s it had increased to nearly 4000 miles, partly by the absorption of smaller companies, but mainly with companies specifically formed by the Chicago and Northwestern holding all their shares and bonds in order to construct new railway lines. Later, once the lines were completed, the company absorbed into its system these proprietary lines as well as various leased ones. The railway's progress had two main objectives: extending westward to the Missouri River and the heart of the grain country, and to the North, reaching the rich mineral belt of upper Michigan with its iron and copper deposits.

Chicago, Portage and Superior Railway Co.

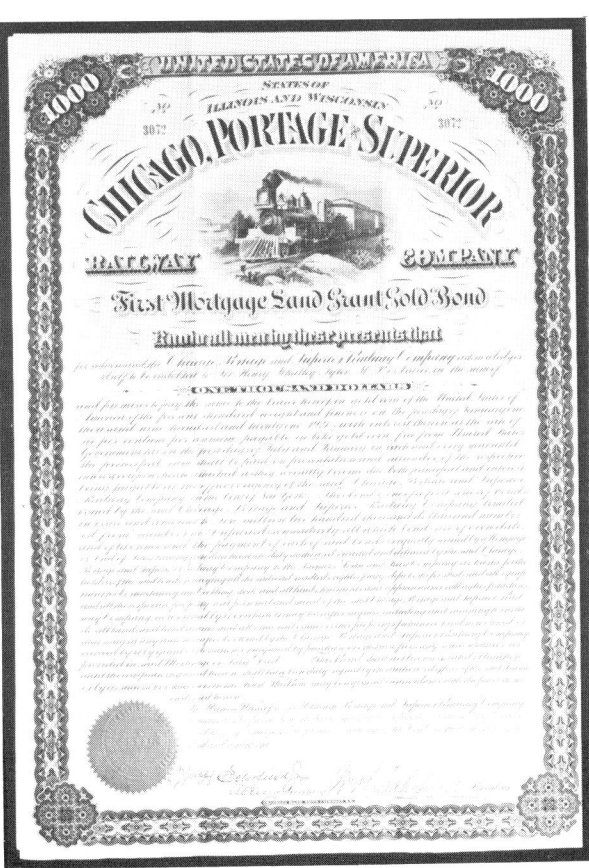

First mortgage land grant six per cent gold bond to bearer for $1000, issued on 1 January 1881 by the Chicago, Portage and Superior Railway Co. chartered in the states of Wisconsin and Illinois. The loan totalled $10,200,000, divided into bonds of $1000, and was secured by a mortgage on the railway company's property, equipment and lands.

Formed in 1873 as a consolidation of several railways, the company was granted by the state of Wisconsin half a million acres of land for extending the line as far as Superior by December 1882, a provision which was duly complied with. In February 1882 the state of Wisconsin transferred the land grant to the Chicago, St. Paul, Minneapolis and Omaha Railway Co.

Chicago, St Paul, Minneapolis and Omaha Railway Co.

Registered certificate for one share of $100 in the common capital stock of the Chicago, St. Paul, Minneapolis and Omaha Railway Co., dated 22 September 1880.

The company was formed on 1 June 1880 by the consolidation of the Chicago, St. Paul and Minneapolis and the North Wisconsin Railway companies.

Cincinnati, Indianapolis, St. Louis and Chicago Railway Co.

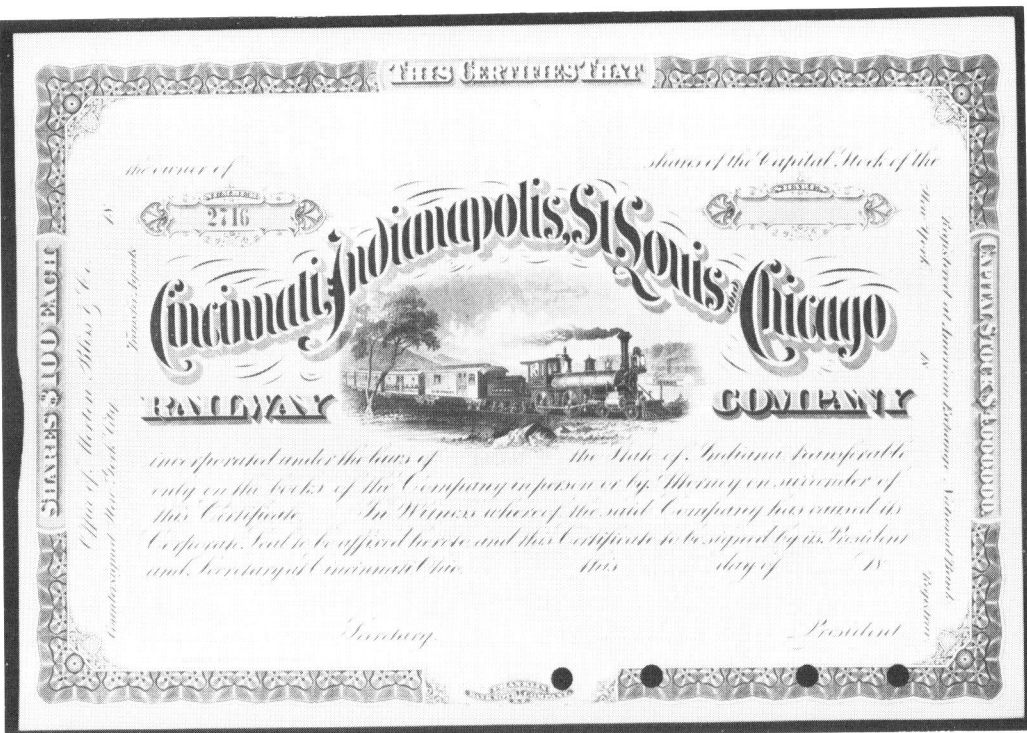

Unissued share certificate of the Cincinnati, Indianapolis, St. Louis and Chicago Railway Co., incorporated in the state of Indiana. The lovely vignette of a steam train passing through a landscape is entitled *View of North Bend, Ohio*.

The company was organised in February 1880 with a share capital of $4 million as successor to the Cincinnati and Indiana Railroad Co. which was sold under foreclosure to the bondholders for $2·5 million. Already in 1881, the company was allowed to increase its share capital to $6 million. Melville E. Ingalls, the prominent railway financier and organiser, held the position of President of the company during the 1880s.

Cincinnati, Sandusky and Cleveland Railroad Co.

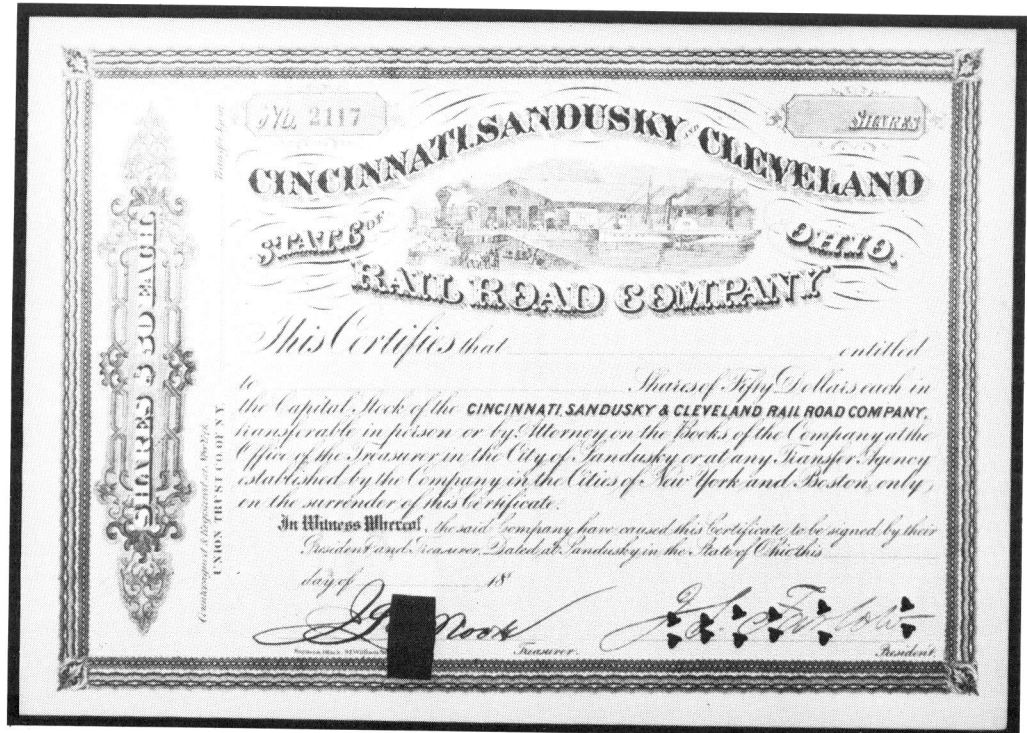

Unissued share certificate of the Cincinnati, Sandusky and Cleveland Railroad Co., which was incorporated in the state of Ohio.

The railway's original charter had been granted in 1832 to the Mad River and Lake Erie Railroad which opened in 1848. In 1870, the company acquired a perpetual lease on the Columbus, Springfield and Cincinnati Railroad, but was in its turn in 1881 leased in perpetuity to the Indiana, Bloomington and Western Railway Co. The certificate bears the signatures of the President, John S. Farlow, and the Treasurer, J. L. Moore, who both held the same posts with the Columbus, Springfield and Cincinnati Railroad Co.

Cincinnati, Wabash and Michigan Railway Co.

Unissued share certificate of the Cincinnati, Wabash and Michigan Railway Co., incorporated in the state of Indiana.

This company was formed as a reorganisation on 14 April 1880 of the Cincinnati, Wabash and Michigan Railroad which went into receivership in 1878 and was sold the following year. Under the terms of the reorganisation of 1880, the share capital was fixed at $3 million, divided into shares of $100 each.

Cincinnati, Washington and Baltimore Railroad Co.

Unissued certificate for 100 shares of $100 each in the preferred capital stock of the Cincinnati, Washington and Baltimore Railroad Co., incorporated in the state of Ohio. Though unissued, the certificate bears the signatures of the Secretary (and auditor) Charles F. Low, and the President, Orland Smith. As a note of interest, the vignette of this certificate, which was printed by the American Banknote Co. in New York, is identical to that of the Baltimore and Ohio Southwestern Railroad.

Orland Smith was followed by William T. McClintick during 1889. In the 1880s another notable figure appeared on the board of directors, namely Robert Garrett who was also President of the Baltimore and Ohio Railroad. The Cincinnati, Washington and Baltimore Railroad Co. was created in 1883 by the reorganisation of various railway companies. Its share capital stood at $21 million of which $13,750,000 formed the preferred stock.

The Cincinnati, Washington and Baltimore Railroad Co.

Registered certificate for 10 shares of $100 each in the common capital stock of the Cincinnati, Washington and Baltimore Railroad Co., dated 5 July 1883 and signed by the President Orland Smith and the Secretary, Charles F. Low. The certificates for the common shares have a different vignette from that on the preferred stock.

The Citizens Passenger Railway Co. (10th & 11th Streets) Pennsylvania

Registered certificate for 10 shares of $50 each in the capital stock of the Citizens Passenger Railway Co., dated 1 February 1866.

The company was incorporated by charter on 25 March 1858 in Philadelphia, Pennsylvania, and started operating a city and suburban tramway on 29 July 1858.

Cleveland, Columbus, Cincinnati and Indianapolis Railway Co.

Registered certificate for 17 shares of $100 each in the capital stock of the Cleveland, Columbus, Cincinnati and Indianapolis Railway Co., dated 1 May 1871.

The company was first chartered on 12 March 1845 under the name of Cleveland, Columbus and Cincinnati Railroad Co. It was completed in February 1851 when trains ran through from Cleveland on Lake Erie to Columbus in Ohio. In 1868, the original company was consolidated with the Bellefontaine Railway Co. under the present name. Its share capital was fixed at $15 million. For 1871 the company paid $3\frac{1}{2}$ per cent dividends.

Cleveland, Columbus, Cincinnati and Indianapolis Railway Co.

Registered certificate for 100 shares of $100 each in the capital stock of the Cleveland, Columbus, Cincinnati and Indianapolis Railway, dated 29 October 1885. In great contrast to the preceding example, the vignette on this certificate shows the role played by the railway in connecting the wheat-growing regions in the West with the industrialised trade ports on the Great Lakes. Between the early 1870s and the mid 1880s, steam navigation had supplanted sailing vessels, although sails were not yet totally phased out.

In 1885 the Cleveland, Columbus, Cincinnati and Indianapolis Railway Co. numbered among its directors Cornelius and William K. Vanderbilt, grandsons of the old Commodore. J. H. Devereux stood as President. The railway became part of the Vanderbilt lines.

(This certificate is illustrated in colour—Plate 2.)

Cleveland, Painsville & Ashtabula Rail Road Co.

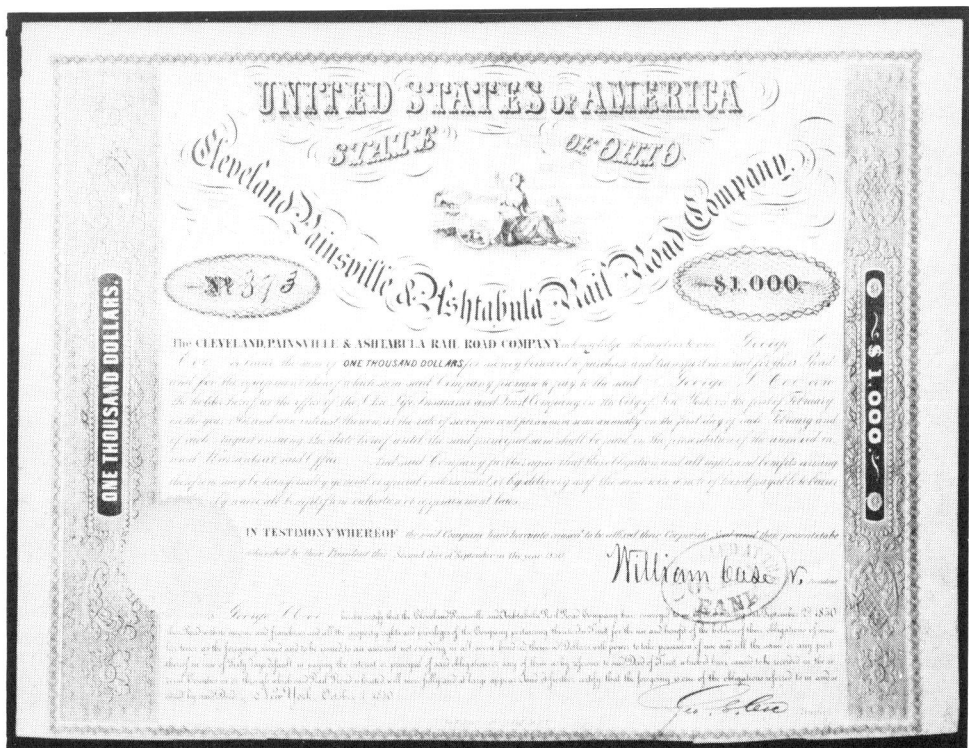

Seven per cent bond to bearer for $1000 issued by the Cleveland, Painsville & Ashtabula Rail Road Co. on 2 September 1850, for redemption in February 1861. The total bond issue was not to exceed $700,000.

Chartered in the state of Ohio in February 1848, the company opened the line in 1852. It underwent a name change in 1868 and was consolidated the following year with other companies as the Lake Shore and Michigan Southern Railway, which in the 1870s was a Vanderbilt line, with Cornelius Vanderbilt as President and his son William as Vice-president.

Cleveland, Painesville and Ashtabula Rail Road Scrip

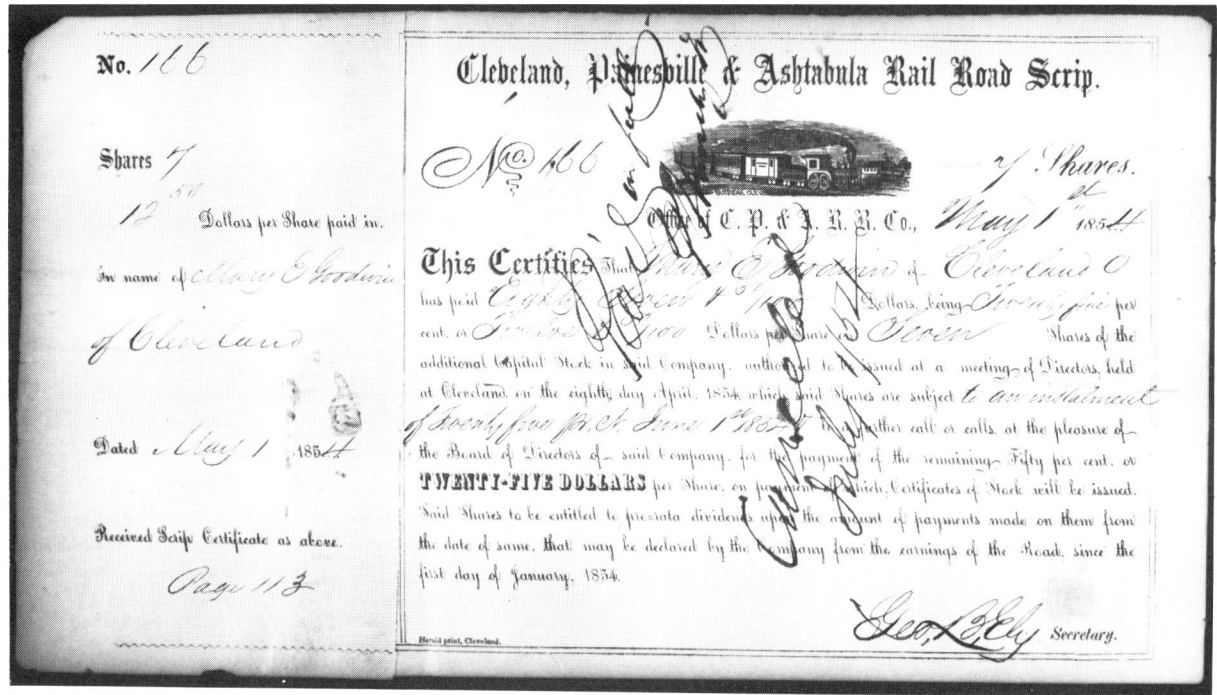

Registered scrip certificate for seven shares in the additional capital stock of the Cleveland, Painesville and Ashtabula Rail Road, dated 1 May 1854. At a meeting of the board held on 8 April 1854, the directors authorized a scrip issue to raise additional capital. The new stock was to be paid for in instalments, starting with a first call of 25 per cent upon which the scrip certificate illustrated here was issued. The next payment of 25 per cent was to be effected on 1 June 1854 and the call for the remainder 50 per cent would be made "at the pleasure of the Board of directors", on payment of which the new share certificates would be issued.

State of Ohio Akron Branch of the Cleveland & Pittsburgh Railroad Co.

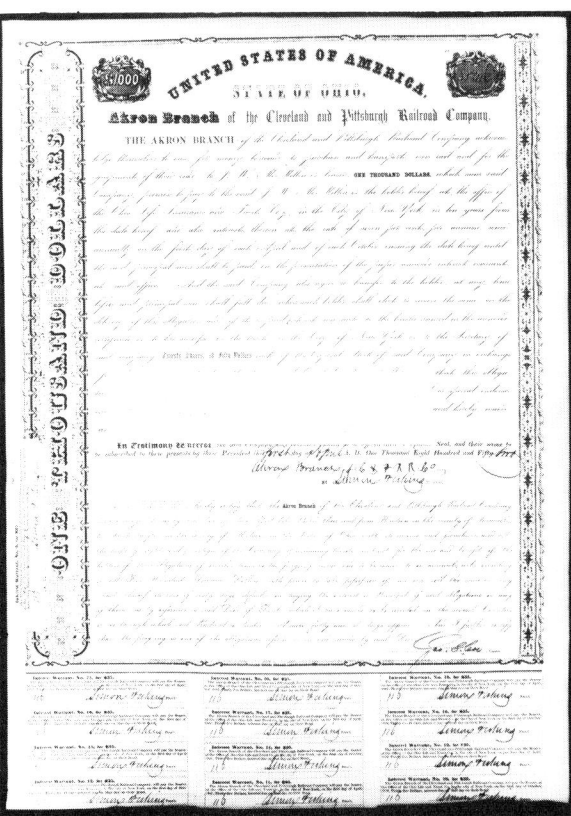

Seven per cent bond to bearer for $1000 issued on 1 April 1852 for redemption in 10 years by the Akron Branch of the Cleveland & Pittsburgh Railroad Co. incorporated in the state of Ohio. The loan was raised to purchase equipment and iron rails for the railway.

First chartered in 1836 in Ohio and in Pennsylvania in 1850, the company opened the line in 1852. Later it was leased to and operated by the Pennsylvania Railroad Co.

Cleveland & Toledo Rail-Road Co.

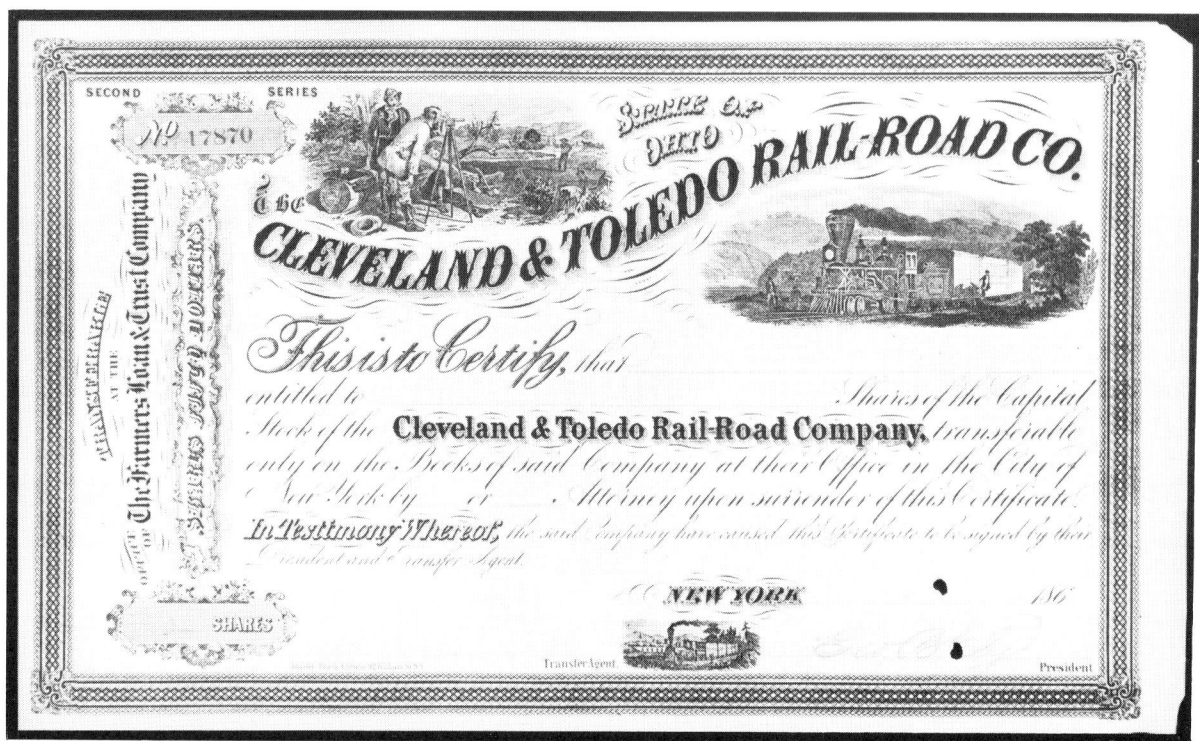

Unissued share certificate of the Cleveland and Toledo Rail-Road Co., incorporated in the state of Ohio.

The company was formed in September 1853 as a consolidation of two earlier ones, the Junction Railroad and the Toledo, Norwalk and Cleveland Railroad. In 1867, the Cleveland and Toledo was leased by the Cleveland, Painesville and Ashtabula Railroad Co. Both were incorporated into the Lake Shore and Michigan Southern Railway in 1869, becoming an integral part of the Vanderbilt lines.

Colorado Midland Railway Co. (State of Colorado)

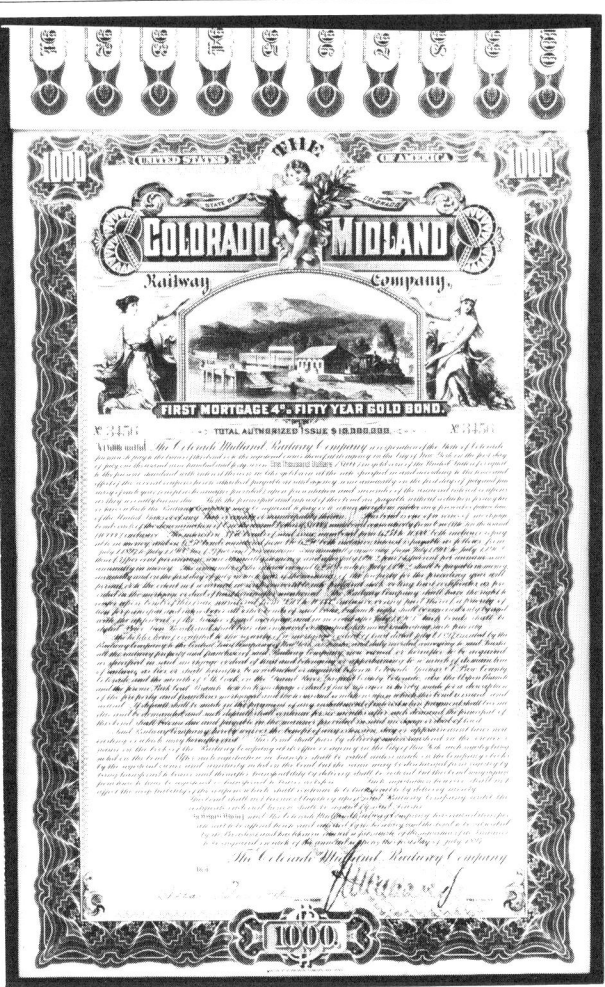

First mortgage four per cent 50 year gold bond for $1000 issued on 1 July 1897 by the Colorado Midland Railway Co., incorporated in the state of Colorado. The authorized bond issue totalled $10 million, divided into bonds of $1000. The loan was secured on the property and equipment of the railway between Colorado Springs and the mouth of Elk Creek on the Rio Grande, as well as the Aspen branch.

During the 1880s, the Colorado Midland was acquired by the Atchison, Topeka & Santa Fé Railroad in the latter's period of expansion. Thanks to similar takeovers and mergers, the Atchison, Topeka & Santa Fé became by 1890 the longest railway in the world, extending to more than 9000 miles. The depression of 1893 badly shook the company which then lost a considerable part of its mileage in the enforced reorganisation. In 1917, the United States District Court of Colorado appointed the Central Trust Co. of New York as trustees against the Colorado Midland Railway. The company was liquidated after a sale under foreclosure in 1918, the bondholders receiving from the trustees $85·55 for each $1000 bond held.

Columbus, Springfield and Cincinnati Rail Road Co.

Unissued share certificate of the Columbus, Springfield and Cincinnati Rail Road Co., incorporated in the state of Ohio.

Formed in 1869 with an issued share capital of $1 million divided into 850 shares, the company opened the line in 1872. It was effectively operated under a perpetual lease by the Cincinnati, Sandusky and Cleveland Railroad, whose President, John S. Farlow, held the same position with the Columbus, Springfield and Cincinnati Railroad during the 1870s.

The Denver and Rio Grande Railroad Co.

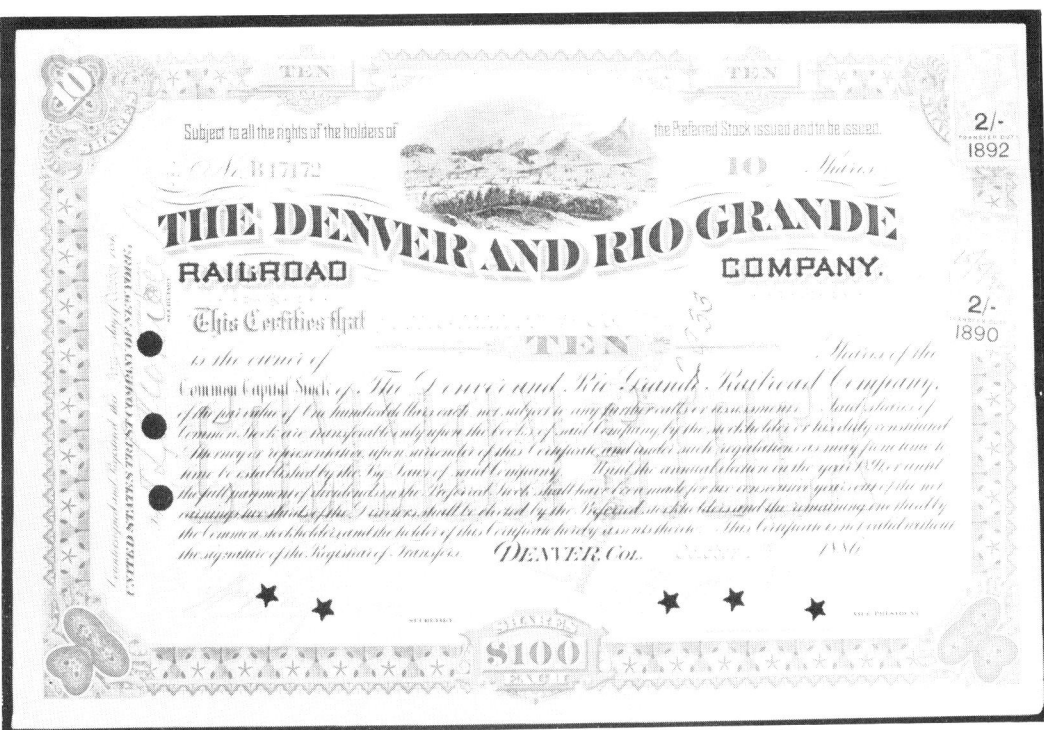

Registered share certificate for 10 shares of $100 each in the common capital stock of the Denver and Rio Grande Railroad Co. The certificate, printed by the American Banknote Co., New York, and bearing a British adhesive revenue stamp in respect of transfer duty, is dated 1 October 1886.

The company was incorporated in the state of Colorado on 27 October 1870 and was granted right of way by Act of Congress in 1871. Construction began at Denver during the same year. In 1872, the line opened from Denver to Pueblo and into the Colorado mountains, where a mining boom had started during the 1870s following the discovery of large deposits of silver, iron and coal. Towards the late 1870s, the Denver and Rio Grande, whose stock had already been purchased by Jay Gould in his plan to acquire a railway empire in the Southwest, was engaged in a merciless rate-slashing competition with rival railway companies. In 1878–1879, the Santa Fé railway, hoping to benefit from the promising returns in the mining boom, invaded Central Colorado, acknowledged to be the territory of the Denver and Rio Grande. The two rival companies fought neck-to-neck in a race to lay down the first track over Royal Gorge to reach the mines. The fight became known as the "canyon war", in which the Denver and Rio Grande lost. As a result, its shares fell heavily on the market. By the time the Supreme Court ruled that no railway could exclude another from a pass, the Sant Fé had bought up its stock and gained control. As for Gould, he had already shed his investment well before October 1884, when the Denver & Rio Grande went into receivership. The company was reorganised in 1885 with the issue of $45,500,000 common shares in exchange for the old stock, in addition to preferred stock and consolidated mortgage bonds. The Santa Fé's victory too was short-lived, as the railway fell into the hands of the receiver in 1893.

The Denver and Rio Grande Railroad Co.

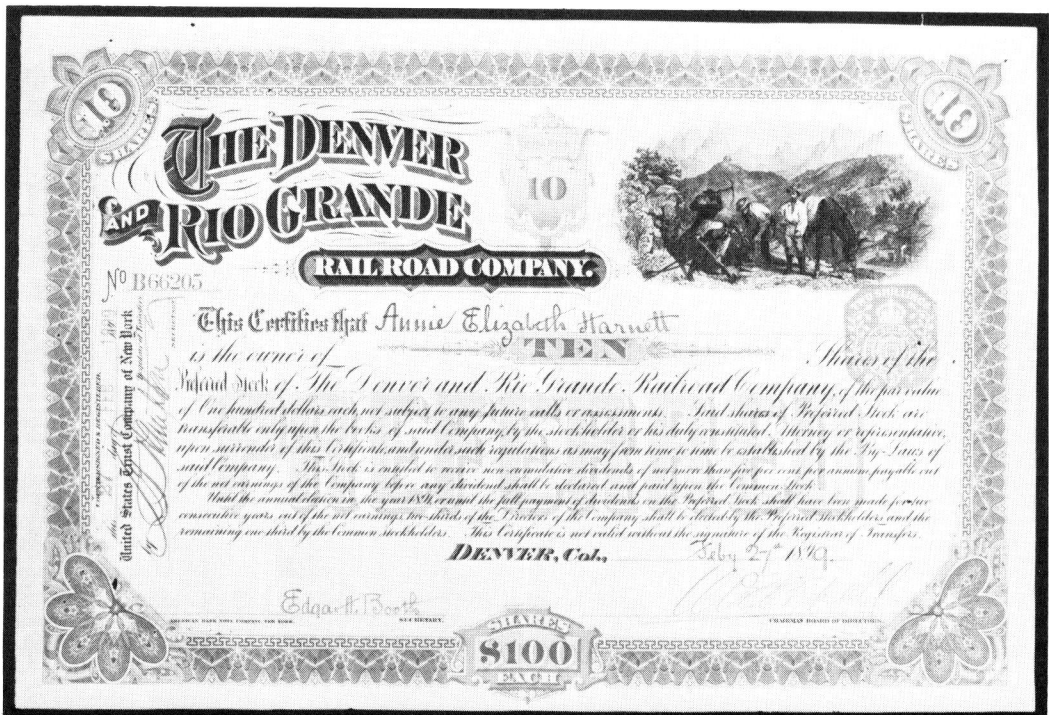

Registered certificate for 10 shares of $100 each in the preferred capital stock of the Denver and Rio Grande Railroad Co., dated 27 February 1899. Differing from the preceding example, the vignette on this later certificate shows a group of mining prospectors.

By 1900, only 50 per cent of the railway companies in the United States could pay dividends. The Denver & Rio Grande Railroad was one of the numerous companies to fall into distress between 1900 and 1920. It was foreclosed more than once and reorganised under the same name.

The Denver and Rio Grande Railroad Co.

This third and more recent registered certificate for 10 shares in the preferred capital stock of the Denver and Rio Grande Railroad Co., dated 6 March 1909 shows again a different design. The single railway line, running along a precipitous and narrow gorge is reminiscent of the fierce battle over Royal Gorge with the Santa Fé Railroad in the race to lay down the track through this deep canyon of the Arkansas River.

Detroit, Grand Rapids and Western Railroad Co.

Registered certificate for 97 shares of $100 each of the preferred capital of the Detroit, Grand Rapids and Western Railroad Co., incorporated in the state of Michigan. The certificate, printed by the American Banknote Co. (New York and Boston), is dated 17 August 1899.

Dubuque & Sioux City Rail Road Co.

Registered certificate for one preferred share of $100 in the capital stock of the Dubuque & Sioux City Rail Road Co., dated 13 September 1867. The authorized preferred capital totalled $2 million.

Chartered by the state of Iowa in November 1856 as the Dubuque and Pacific Railroad Co., it went into receivership in 1860, with barely 80 miles of the railway completed. After the foreclosure, a new company was formed under the present name. Less than a month after this certificate was issued, the Illinois Central Railroad leased the railway for twenty years at a rental of 35 per cent of gross earnings for the first 10 years and 36 per cent for the remainder. During this period, John P. Morgan stood as a director of the company.

Eastern & Western Air Line Railway Co.

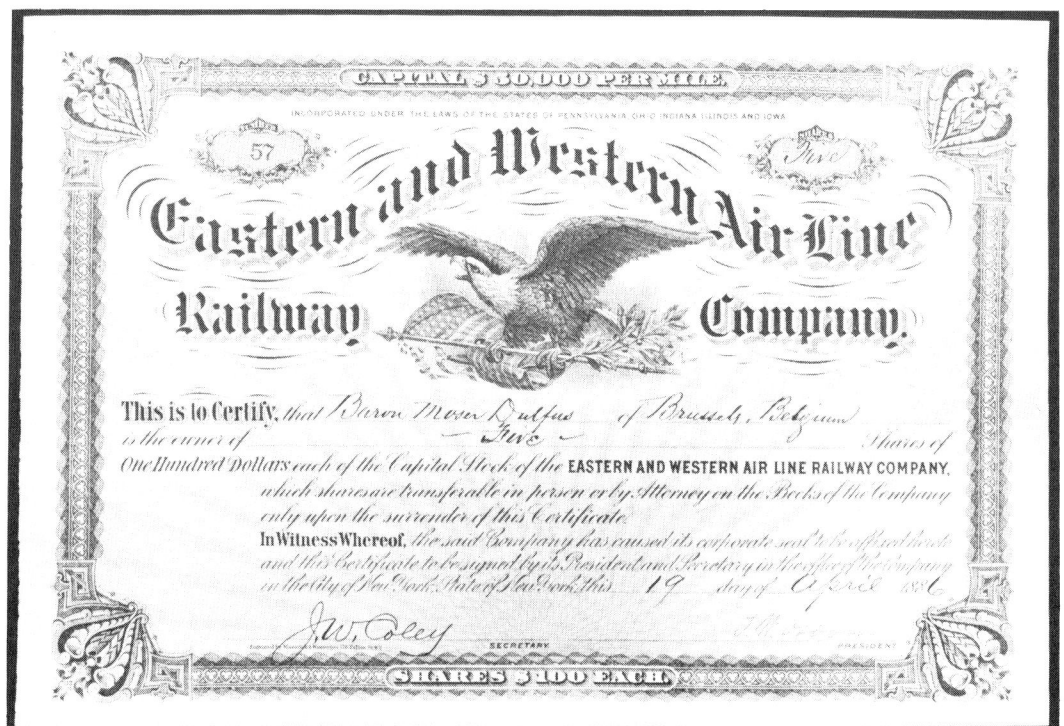

Registered certificate for five shares of $100 each in the capital stock of the Eastern and Western Air Line Railway Co., dated 19 April 1886.

The company was formed in December 1884 as a consolidation of several companies bearing the same name which had been chartered earlier in the year by the states of Pennsylvania, Ohio, Indiana, Illinois and Iowa. These charters authorized the construction of a railway from Punxutawney in Pennsylvania to Council Bluffs, Iowa, with a branch to Chicago. The authorized share capital amounted to $52,600,000, which represented approximately $50,000 per mile.

The Electric Traction Co. of Philadelphia

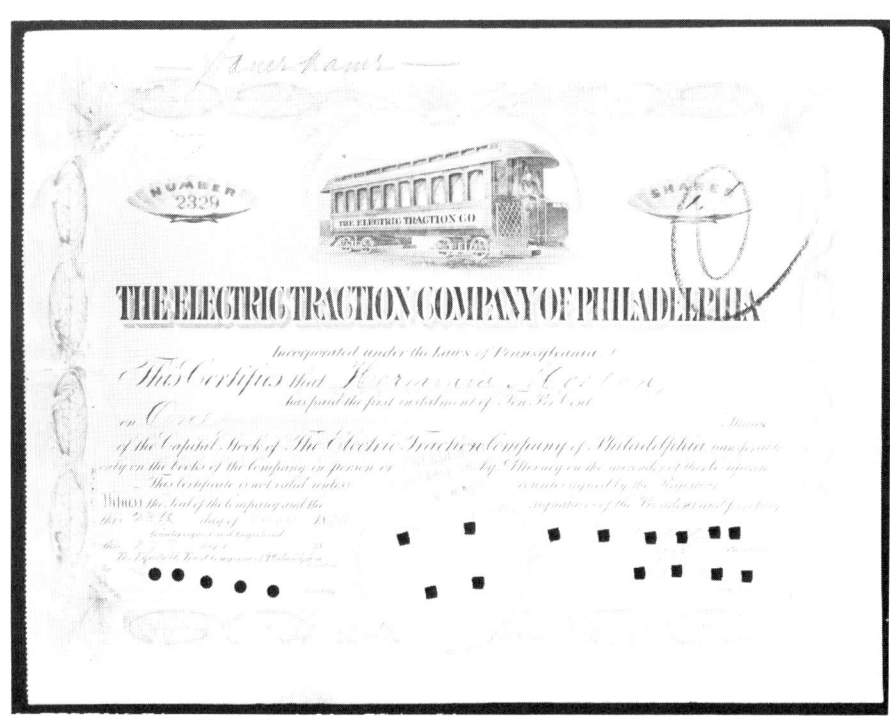

Registered certificate for one partly paid share in the capital stock of The Electric Traction Co. of Philadelphia, incorporated in Pennsylvania in May 1893. This certificate was issued after payment of a first instalment of 10 per cent on 28 June 1894 and was cancelled in July 1895 by the registrars.

Electric tramways started to replace the old street horse-drawn tramways in the early 1890s.

Erie Railroad Co.

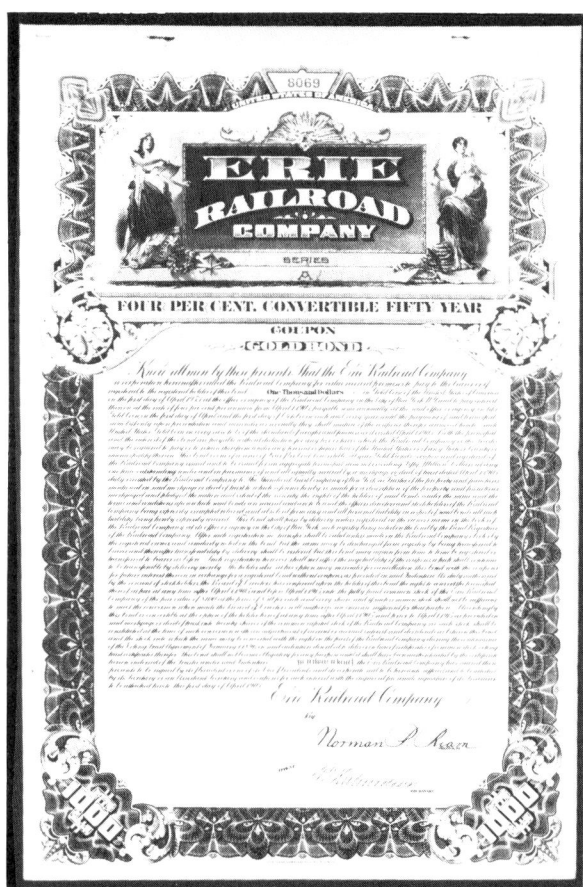

Four per cent 50 year gold bond to bearer for $1000, issued by the Erie Railroad Co. on 1 April 1903. The bonds, on which both the principal and the interest were paid free of taxes, formed part of an issue not exceeding $50 million and were convertible between 1905 and 1915 into ordinary shares of the company at the rate of $50 per $100 share, thus entitling the holder of a $1000 bond to 20 shares of $100 in the common stock. The certificate was printed by the International Banknote Co., New York.

From its inception the Erie Railroad was bedevilled by ills and misfortunes of all kinds. The company's charter, granted by the state of New York in April 1832, authorized the construction of a line from the Hudson River to the Lakes to meet the needs of New York City and the southern part of New York state. Eventually after a series of delays and financial embarrassments, the line was completed and opened in 1851. It was an ambitious project at that time, since no railway had ever been built on such a large scale. Unfortunately, due to political reasons the railway did not gain a direct access into New York City nor did it reach any of the major ports on Lake Erie. Because of chronic financial difficulties it passed into the hands of a receiver no less than four times in the first 30 years of its existence. Probably the most notorious period for the railway was during the years when it was managed by Daniel Drew, then from 1867 till 1872 by Jay Gould, starting his career as a railway financier and helped by the flamboyant James Fisk, who had selected as company headquarters the premises of New York's Grand Opera House. In the acrimonious fight for control of the Erie with Cornelius Vanderbilt during 1867-68, the long-suffering company was brought to near disaster by the gang's wild share manipulations, illegal issues of "watered" stock and ruinous rate-slashing war against its rival. Gould's departure however did not signify that troubles for the Erie Railroad were over. Again it fell into the hands of a receiver and was reorganized in 1887 as the New York Lake Erie and Western Railroad, which in its turn defaulted and was reconstructed in 1895 as the Erie Railroad.

Escanaba, Iron Mountain and Western Rail Road Co. (State of Michigan)

Five per cent 30 year first mortgage gold bond to bearer for $1000, issued on 1 November 1890 by the Escanaba, Iron Mountain and Western Rail Road Co., incorporated in the state of Michigan. The certificate was printed by the American Banknote Co., New York.

To finance the construction of a railway from Escanaba on Lake Michigan westwards to Iron Mountain, which was in 1890 a small town with a population of 8500 inhabitants, the centre of a region rich in mineral deposits, bonds were issued at the rate of $25,000 per constructed mile, secured on the railway's franchise, property and equipment.

Evansville and Terre Haute Railroad Co. (State of Indiana)

Consolidated six per cent 30 year first mortgage bond to bearer for $1000 of the Evansville and Terre Haute Railroad Co., dated 1 June 1880. This bond was one of a series of 1500 bonds of $1000 each, secured by a mortgage on the franchises and property belonging to the main line of the railway company. Although the bond bears the company seal and the signature of the secretary, it was not issued, as the president's signature is lacking. The certificate was printed by the Franklin Banknote Co., New York.

Incorporated in the state of Indiana, the company was first known as the Evansville and Crawfordsville Railroad Co. whose line opened in 1854. The name of Evansville and Terre Haute Railroad Co. was adopted in 1877.

Fair Haven & Westville Rail Road Co.

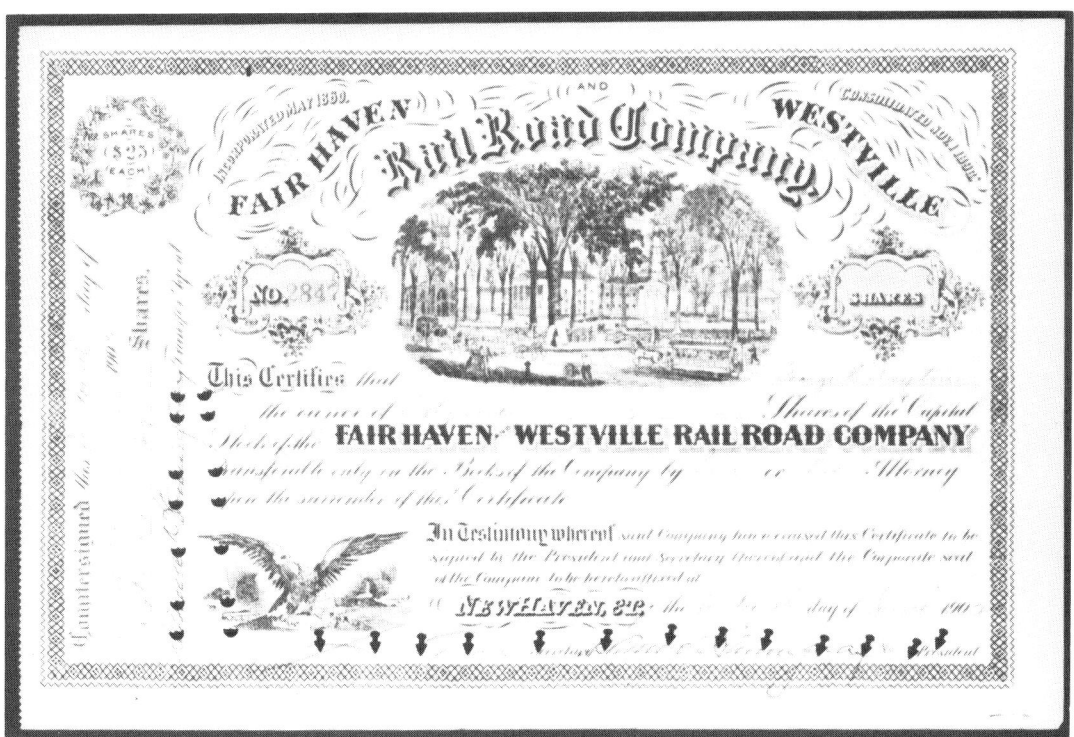

Registered certificate for 67 shares of $25 each in the Fair Haven & Westville Railroad Co. dated 14 June 1902.

Incorporated in the state of Connecticut in 1860 and consolidated in November 1898, the company operated a city and suburban tramway of some seven miles in length.

Fitchburg & Worcester Rail Road Co.

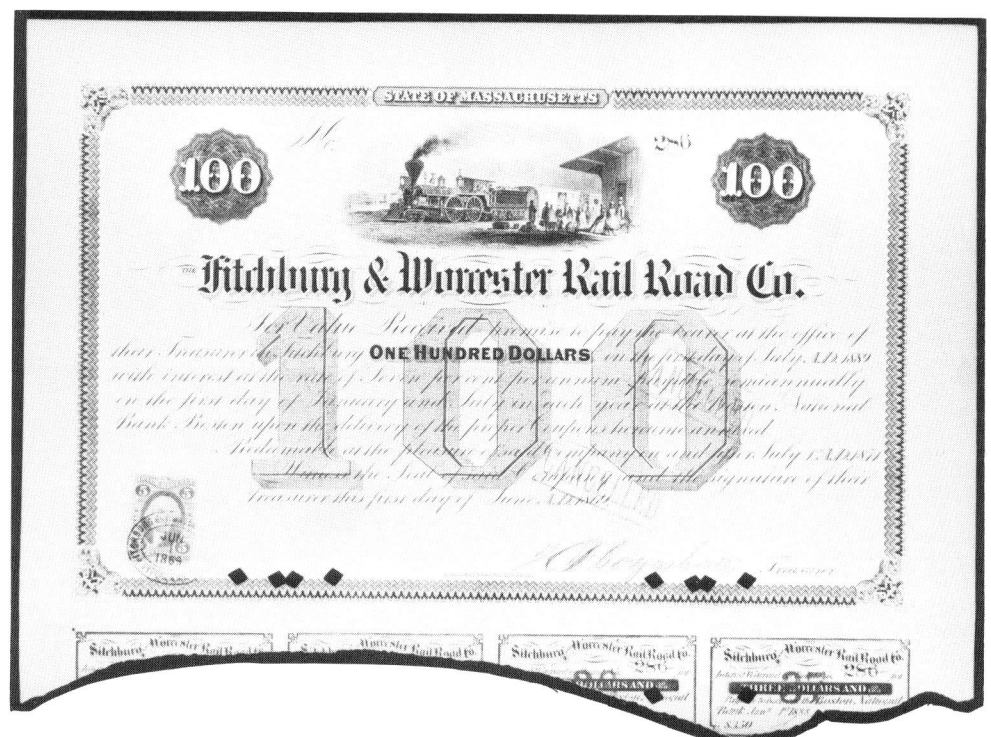

Seven per cent 20 year bond to bearer for $100, issued on 1 June 1869 by the Fitchburg & Worcester Railroad Co. This certificate was printed by the American Banknote Co.

The railway, opened in 1850, consisted of some 42 miles of line. Chartered by the state of Massachusetts in 1846, the company was consolidated on 1 July 1869, just one month after the bond issue, into the Boston, Clinton and Fitchburg Railroad.

Flint and Pere Marquette Railway Co.

Registered certificate for 12 shares of $100 each in the Flint and Pere Marquette Railway Co., dated 25 June 1872. The certificate was printed by Henry Seibert and Bros., Ledger Building, Cox, William and Spruce St., New York.

Chartered by the state of Michigan in 1857, the company was consolidated on 4 June 1872 with three other railway companies. The 280 miles of line were completed in 1874. The company divided the land grants it had received from the state into several trusts to secure mortgages.

Flint and Pere Marquette Railroad Co.

After defaulting on the payment of interest on its consolidated bonds, the Flint and Pere Marquette Railroad Co. was put into receivership in 1879 and sold under foreclosure in 1880 to a committee of the consolidated mortgage bondholders who reorganised it on 31 August 1880. According to the reconstruction scheme, the total share capital authorized amounted to $10 million, of which $6,500,000 represented the preferred capital. The share certificate of 16 February 1883 illustrated here shows a change in the design of the share after the reorganisation.

Fort Wayne & Belle Isle Railway Co.

Registered certificate for one share of $100 in the Fort Wayne and Belle Isle Railway Co., dated 20 June 1892. After the share changed hands, this certificate was cancelled by the company secretary in 1895 and exchanged for a new one.

The company was incorporated during the same year in the state of Michigan with an authorized share capital of $250,000. The company operated a city and suburban electric tramway.

Fort Wayne, Cincinnati and Louisville Railroad Co.

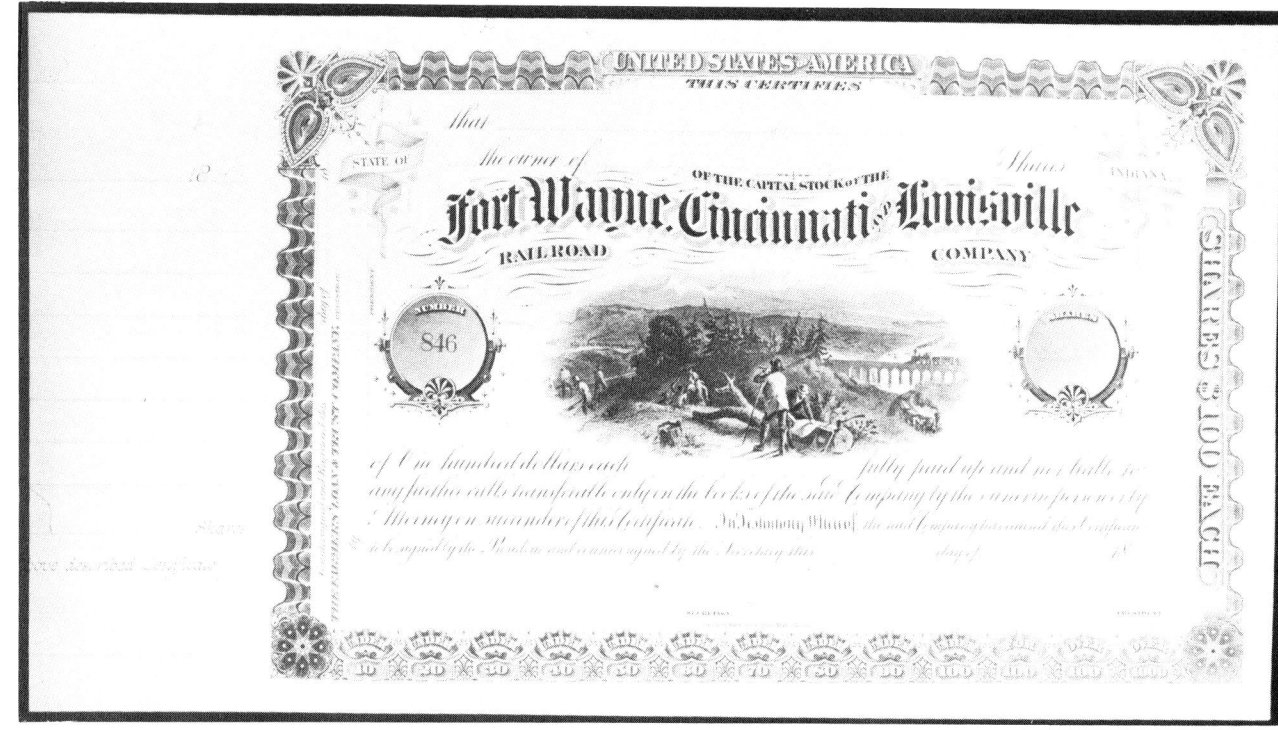

Unissued share certificate of the Fort Wayne, Cincinnati and Louisville Railroad Co., incorporated in the state of Indiana.

The interesting vignette, which also appears on the share certificate of the Keokuk and Des Moines Railway Co., shows the rapid progress of railways in the country. Three trains can be seen travelling through the hilly landscape. In the foreground of the picture, two surveyors are busy measuring land while a group of railway labourers are laying down a new track on the left. In the centre, a small party of Indians, probably feeling threatened by this invasion of their territory, seem to be taking to flight. The penetration and occupation of Indian-occupied lands was made much faster by the advance of the railways in the West, which the Indians were powerless to resist. The certificate was printed by the American Banknote Co., New York and Boston.

This railway, which opened in 1870 under the name of Fort Wayne, Muncie and Cincinnati Railroad, was placed under receivership after defaulting on the payment of interest on its bonds and sold under foreclosure in 1881 to a committee of bondholders for $1 million. They subsequently reorganised it as the Fort Wayne, Cincinnati and Louisville Railroad with an issued share capital of $4 million.

Georgia Rail Road & Banking Co.

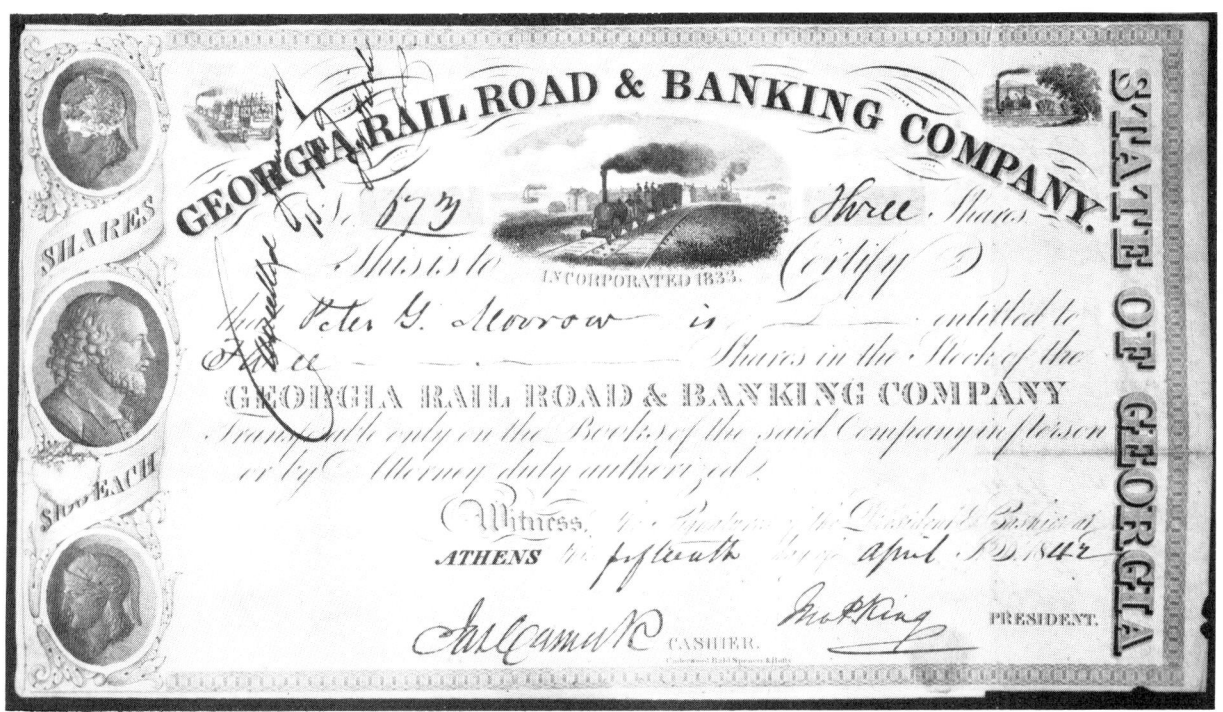

Early registered certificate for three shares of $100 each in the Georgia Rail Road and Banking Co., dated 15 April 1842. Attached to the certificate is a transfer document signed by the shareholder empowering his attorney to sell his holdings to a third party, in accordance with the company's provisions that the shares are "Transferable only on the Books of the said Company in person or by Attorney duly authorized". The two red blotches in the left-hand margins are fragments of the company's wax seals. The certificate was printed by Underwood Bald Spencer and Huffy.

Incorporated in the state of Georgia in December 1833 as the Georgia Railroad Co., it changed its name to Georgia Rail Road and Banking Co., in 1835, and opened a line from Augusta to Atlanta in 1837. The Georgia Railroad was one of the first lines to be built in the Southern states, where railway development began later and progressed slower than in the North where much larger capital resources were available. The construction of many Southern railways was financed by railbanks, organised on the principle of interlocking directorates by which the affairs of the railway company and of the bank were closely linked with the aim of protecting both corporations in times of stress. Shareholders of the railway company became also holders of the bank stock at par, but while the bank was not responsible for any losses of the railway company, the latter was responsible for any debts of the bank. Despite the inherent risks of such a system, many railways were successfully financed by it and survived.

Germantown Passenger Rail Way Co.

Registered certificate for one share of $50 in the Germantown Passenger Rail Way Co., dated 20 November 1894.

The company, incorporated in Philadelphia, Pennsylvania, operated a city tramway, originally horse-drawn. The issued share capital stood at $1,500,000.

Grand Junction Rail Road & Depot Co. (Massachusetts)

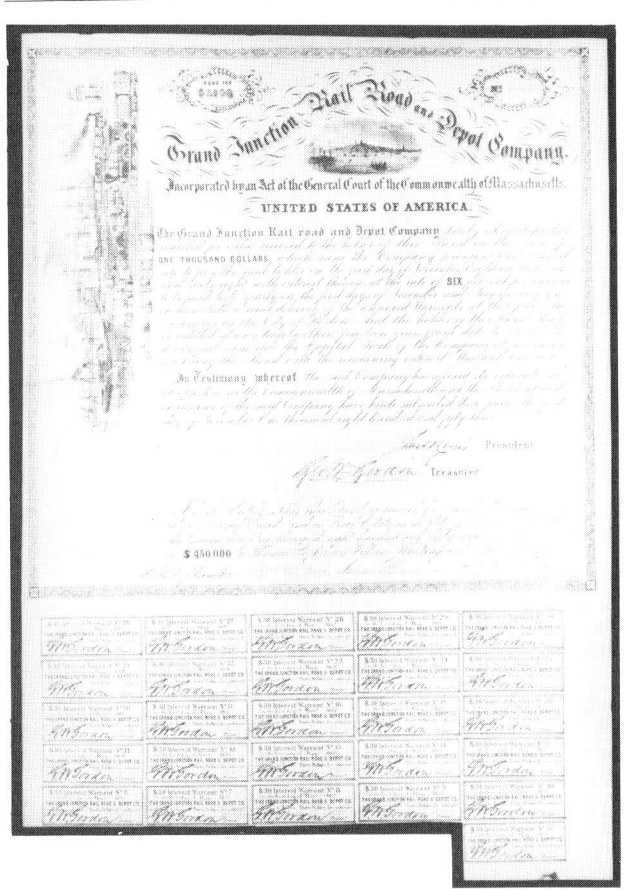

Fourteen year convertible second mortgage six per cent bond to bearer for $1000 issued on 1 November 1853 by the Grand Junction Rail Road & Depot Co. incorporated in Boston, Massachusetts, in 1847. The bonds were secured by a second mortgage on the Union Rail Road, a street railway in Boston, and on real estate in the city, for the sum of $450,000.

The elaborate vignette on the side of the certificate shows a view of Boston Harbout bustling with activity. A paddle steamer entering the harbour is making for the embarkation quay where a crowd stands ready to board, while goods are waiting to be loaded on a nearby train. Through the billowing smoke from the ships' funnels and the steam engines, one distinguishes also the tall masts of several clippers and schooners mingling with the steamships. The certificate was engraved by Morge and Tuttle.

The Grand River Valley Railroad Co.

Unissued share certificate of The Grand River Valley Railroad Co. The certificate was engraved by the American Banknote Co., New York.

Chartered by the state of Michigan in 1846, the company opened the 84 miles of line from Jackson to Grand Rapids in 1870. Leased in perpetuity to the Michigan Central Railroad Co. which also operated it, the Grand River Valley Railroad was re-incorporated on 25 April 1894 with an authorized share capital of $1 million, divided into 10000 shares of $100 each of which only 4912 were issued. The Michigan Central Railroad paid an annual rent of five per cent on the issued amount of $491,200.

The Greenville & Columbia Rail Road Co.

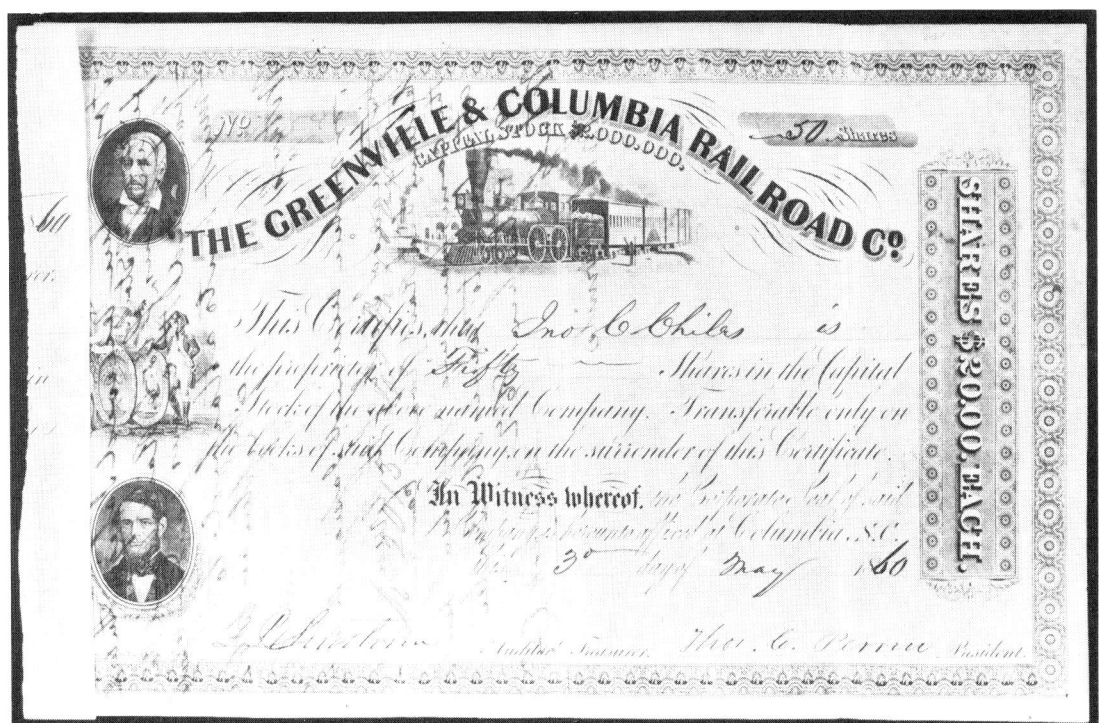

Registered certificate for 50 shares of $20 each in The Greenville & Columbia Rail Road Co., dated 3 May 1860. The certificate was printed by Rawdon, Wright, Hatch and Edson, New York.

Numbering ammong the early Southern railway companies, it was chartered by South Carolina in December 1846. The line from Greenville to Columbia, a distance of 142 miles, was opened in December 1853. The authorized share capital amounted to $2 million.

Gulf, Mobile and Northern Railroad Co.

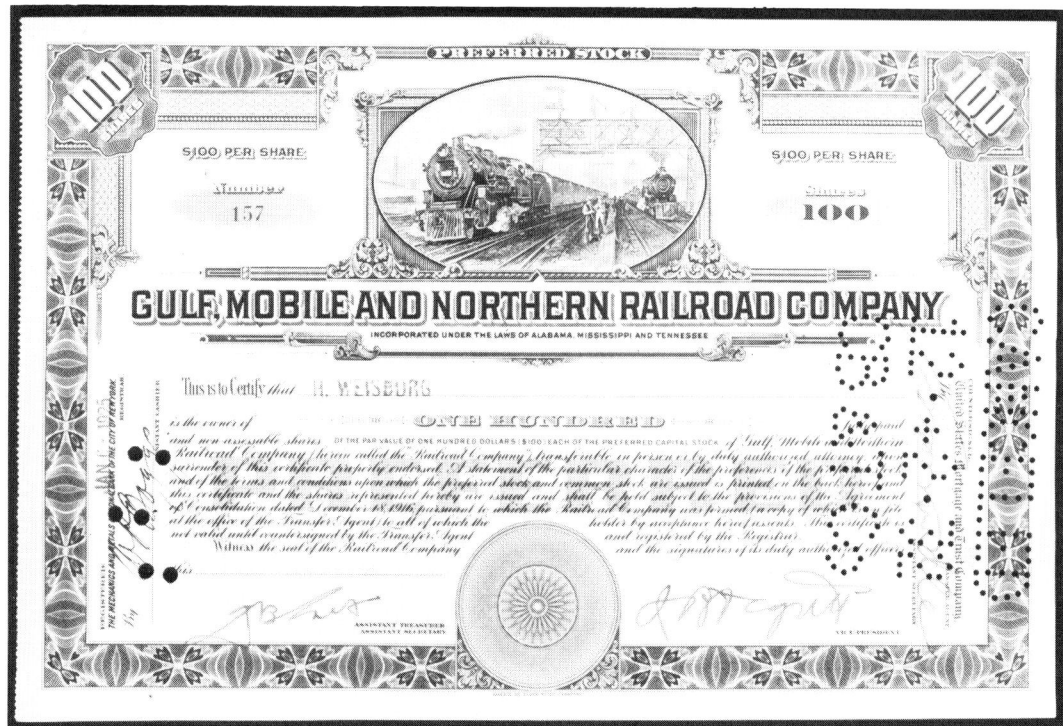

Registered certificate for 100 shares of $100 each in the preferred capital stock of the Gulf, Mobile and Northern Railroad Co., dated 5 January 1925. The certificate was engraved by the American Banknote Co.

The company was incorporated in the states of Alabama, Mississipi and Tennessee as a consolidation on 18 December 1916. The company was controlled and operated under lease by the Illinois Central Railroad from 1933. In 1940 it merged into the Gulf, Mobile & Ohio Railroad.

Gulf, Mobile & Ohio Railroad Co.

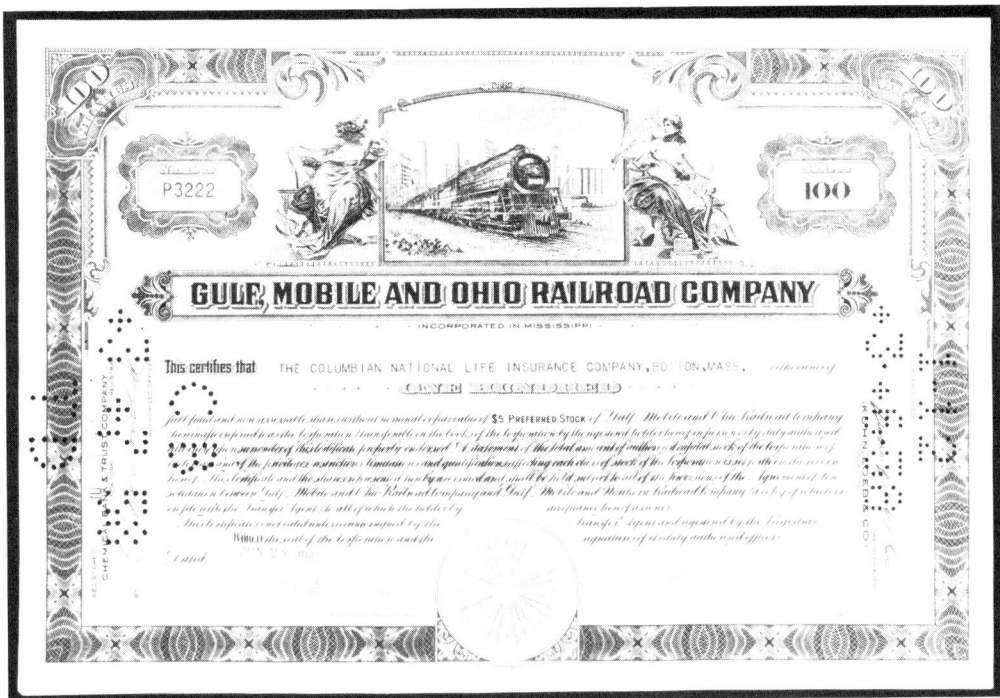

Registered certificate for one hundred shares without nominal value in the $5 preferred stock of the Gulf, Mobile & Ohio Railroad Co., dated 23 June 1941. The certificate was engraved by the Security Banknote Co.

The company, incorporated in the state of Mississipi in 1938, was consolidated with the Gulf, Mobile & Northern Railroad Co. in 1940. The agreement provided for an issue of 915,597 shares without par value, of which 305,750 shares constituted the $5 preferred stock, i.e., holders of preference shares were entitled to dividends at the rate of $5 per share. On 10 August 1972, the Gulf, Mobile & Ohio Railroad and the Illinois Central Railroad formally merged to form a new system, the Illinois Central Gulf Railroad Co., a wholly-owned subsidiary of Illinois Central Industries, Inc. Under the terms of the merger, shareholders received 0·75 share of the new stock for each common share held.

Harrisburg Railways Co.

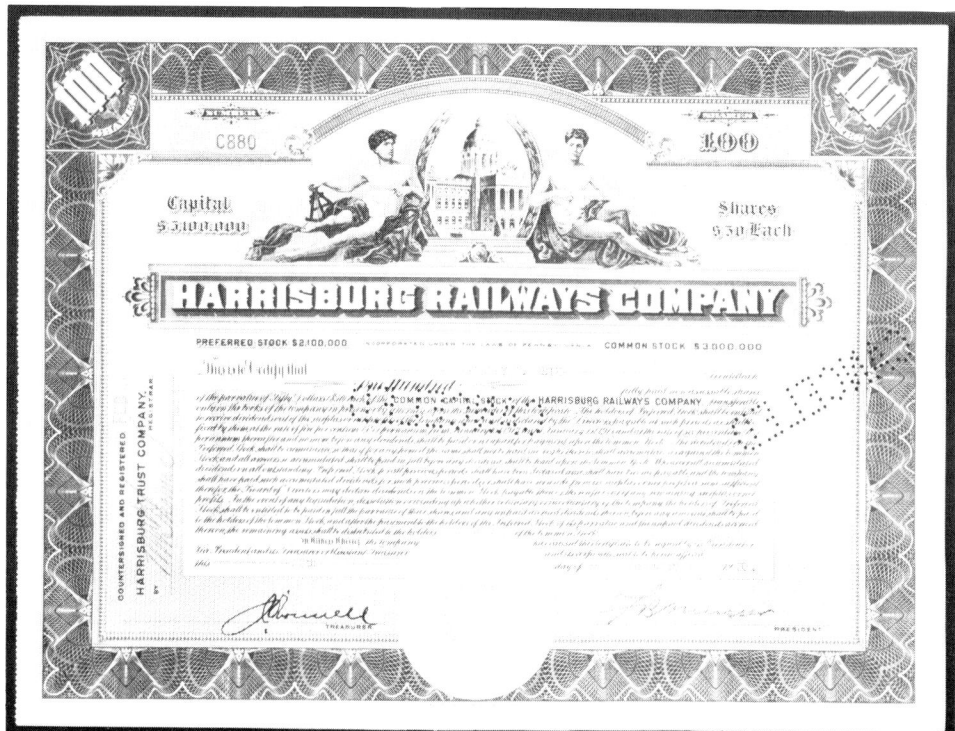

Registered certificate for 100 shares of $50 each in the common stock of the Harrisburg Railways Co., dated 20 February 1930. The certificate was printed by the Security Banknote Co., Philadelphia.

The company was incorporated in the state of Pennsylvania on 29 November 1912 with a total share capital of $5,100,000, of which $2,100,000 formed the preferred stock and $3 million the common stock.

Hartford and Connecticut Valley Railroad Co.

Registered certificate for 16 shares of $100 in the capital stock of the Hartford and Connecticut Valley Railroad Co., dated 31 August 1882.

The original charter of the company, which was then called the Connecticut Valley Railroad, was granted in July 1868. The whole line opened in 1872 from Hartford to Fenwick, in Connecticut, a distance of 46 miles. A reorganisation took place in March 1879 when the company adopted the present name. At the end of 1882, the New York, New Haven and Hartford Railroad Co. acquired a controlling interest in the company's capital stock.

Hartford and Connecticut Western Railroad Co.

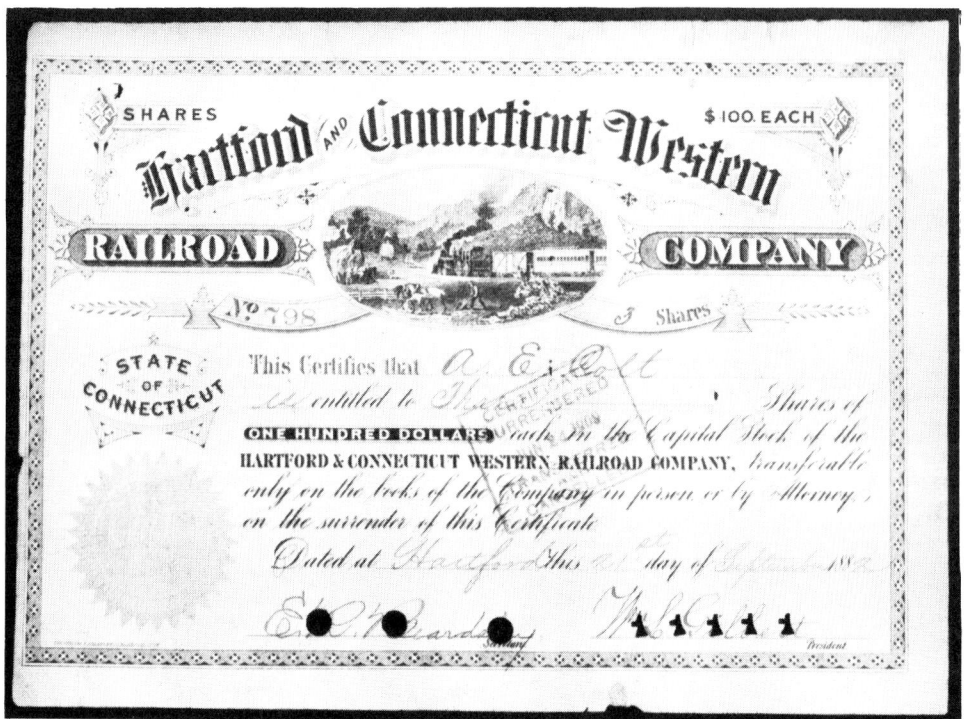

Registered certificate for three shares of $100 each in the Hartford and Connecticut Western Railroad Co. dated 21 September 1882.

The Company, chartered by the state of Connecticut in 1868, opened the 108 miles of line from Hartford to Rhinecliffe, in New York, in 1871. Having fallen into difficulties by the late 1870s, it was operated from 1880 to August 1881 by the Connecticut State Treasurer until a new reorganised company was formed. Under the terms of the reorganisation, bonds of the old company were exchanged for stock in the new company on the basis of 60 per cent of their par value.

Hudson & Manhattan Railroad Co.

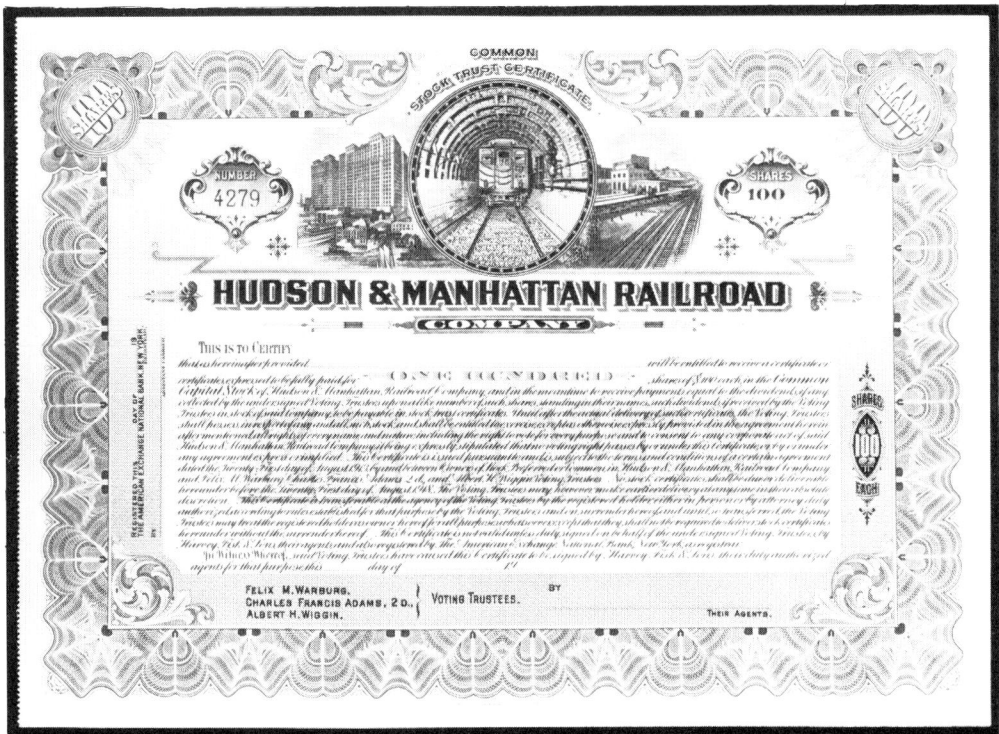

This unissued trust certificate entitled the holder to receive a certificate for 100 shares in the common stock of the Hudson & Manhattan Railroad Co. From 1 August 1913, the company was controlled by a group of voting trustees, one of which was Felix M. Warburg, a banker of German origin and partner of Kuhn, Loeb & Co., in New York. The vignette on this certificate, engraved by the Republic Banknote Co., Pittsburgh, shows a sectional view of the railway tunnel under the Hudson River.

Hudson & Manhattan Railroad Co.

Registered share certificate for 100 shares of $100 each in the preferred stock of the Hudson & Manhattan Railroad Co., dated 21 April 1947.

The company was incorporated in the state of New York and New Jersey in 1906 with an authorized capital of $10 million preferred stock and $50 million common stock. From 1 July 1911, the preferred stock became, at the option of the holder, convertible into common stock at $110 per share. The vignette on this certificate, engraved by the American Banknote Co., New York, shows a sectional view of a train crossing the Hudson River by underwater tunnel. The company was reorganised on 31 December 1961 with no shareholders' equity as the Hudson & Manhattan Corporation whose liquidation was completed in 1974 with the distribution of the final payment.

Illinois and Fox River Central Railroad Co.

First mortgage five per cent 20 year gold bond to bearer for $500, issued on 1 June 1907 by the Illinois and Fox River Central Railroad Co., incorporated in the state of Illinois. The total issue amounted to $2,500,000 divided into 1000 bonds of $500 and 2000 bonds of $1000. The certificate illustrated here bears the serial number 5. The mortgage was secured on the company's railway lines from Ottawa (Illinois) to Chicago, Yorkville (Illinois) to Morris (Illinois) and its Sheridan branch. The certificate, on which the company's ornate gold seal was affixed, was engraved by the Western Banknote Co., Chicago.

Illinois Central Rail Road Co.

Registered certificate for 16 shares of $100 each in the Illinois Central Rail Road Co., dated 21 February 1919. The certificate, engraved by the American Banknote Co., New York, shows a map of the railway's extensive network.

The company's charter was granted in February 1851 by the state of Illinois which also conferred on it the right of way and land grants received in 1850 from Congress 'for building a railroad from Chicago to Mobile'. The charter provided that the company should pay the state, in lieu of taxes, seven per cent of the gross earnings of the original line, which was completed in 1856. In the following decades, the Illinois Central extended its network into neighbouring states, aiming to carry out the ambitious plan of linking the Great Lakes to the Gulf of Mexico. Several companies were acquired or leased for the construction and operation of the new lines. In 1883, Edward H. Harriman, then a young stockbroker and banker, was brought in as a director of the company. Throughout the 1890s, together with President Stuyvesant Fish, he followed a policy of further expansion, extending the mileage of the railway by new acquisitions and leases in order to increase business. During the first decade of the twentieth century, the Illinois Central carried out a concerted policy of improvement in plant and equipment while acquiring new lines to bring the Illinois Central south, particularly as the south-eastern regions of the United States were experiencing a substantial industrial and agricultural growth.

Illinois Central Railroad Co.

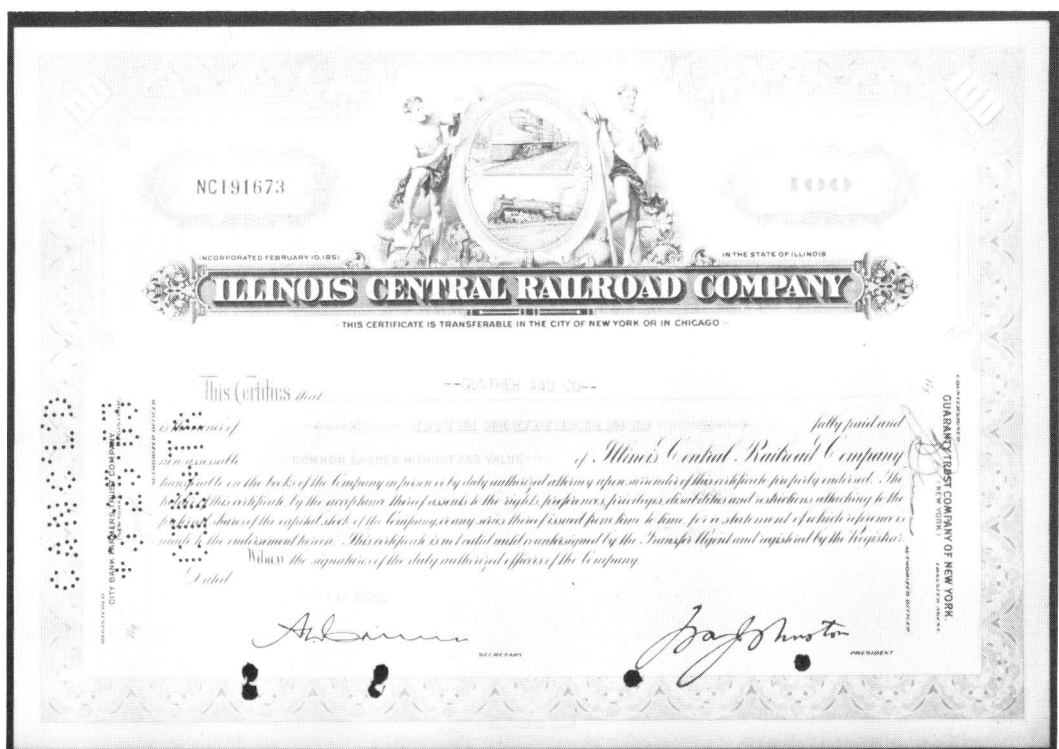

A recent example, this registered certificate for 100 common shares without par value in the Illinois Central Railroad Co. is dated 8 June 1954 and bears the facsimile signature of the president at that time, Wayne Johnston. The company was recapitalised in 1954, with the common shares of $100 changed to no par value and one additional share issued. In 1972, it merged into Illinois Central Industries Inc., each common share no par being exchanged for three common no par shares. Different from the preceding one, the vignette on this certificate engraved by the American Banknote Co. depicts contemporary express locomotives.

Indianapolis & Cincinnati Rail Road Co.

Unissued share certificate of the Indianapolis & Cincinnati Rail Road Co., chartered by the state of Indiana. Except for its title, the artwork, vignettes and the wording of the document are in all respects identical to the shares of another company, the Indianapolis, Cincinnati and Lafayette Railroad Co. This certificate was printed by Rawdon, Wright, Hatch and Edson, Cincinnati and New York.

The Indianapolis and Cincinnati Railroad Co. was formed in 1861, and the railway was opened in 1866. It was leased in perpetuity to the Indianapolis, Cincinnati and Lafayette Railroad.

Indianapolis, Cincinnati and Lafayette Rail Road Co.

Unissued share certificate of the Indianapolis, Cincinnati and Lafayette Rail Road Co., identical in all parts except for the title and the president's signature, to the unissued certificate of the Indianapolis and Cincinnati Rail Road Co. illustrated previously. This certificate was printed by the American Banknote Co., New York.

Chartered by the state of Indiana, the Indianapolis, Cincinnati and Lafayette Railroad opened in 1852. During the 1870s its affairs were run by Melville E. Ingalls, one of the great railway financiers and entrepreneurs, who was president at that time.

The Ithaca, Auburn and Western Railway Co.

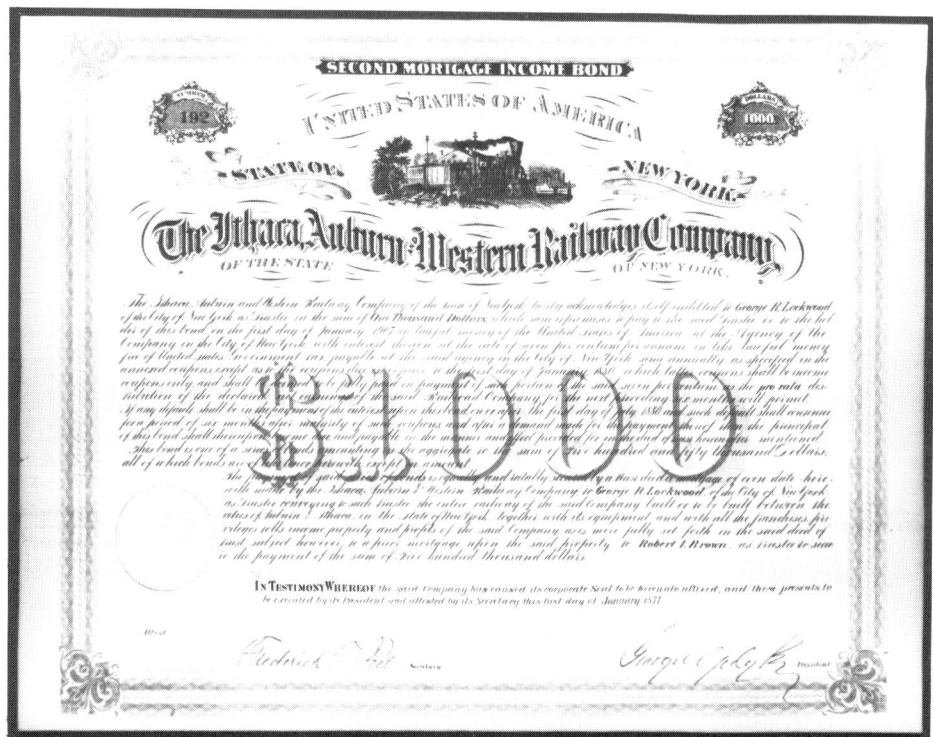

Second mortgage seven per cent income bond to bearer for $1000 for redemption after 30 years, issued by The Ithaca, Auburn and Western Railway Co. on 1 January 1877. This certificate was engraved by Morrison and Bisland, Stationers, 38 New St., New York.

The railway company, which was formed in 1876 in the state of New York as successor to the western extension of the New York and Oswego Midland Railroad Co., raised a second mortgage secured on the railway's franchises, property and equipment in order to finance the construction or completion of the line between Auburn and Ithaca. The total issue amounted to $500,000.

Junction Rail Road Co.

Unissued share certificate of the Junction Rail Road Co., which had been granted a perpetual charter by the state of Ohio. However, the company went into receivership and was foreclosed in 1872. The certificate illustrated here was printed by Snyder & Black, 87 Fulton St., New York.

The Kanawha and Michigan Railway Co.

Unissued share certificate for use in the early 1900s of The Kanawha and Michigan Railway Co. The issued share capital of this company, that it was organised as a successor to the Kanawha and Ohio Railway Co. which was sold under foreclosure in 1890. This certificate was printed by the American Banknote Co., New York.

The Kansas City Railways Co.

Second mortgage five per cent gold bond to bearer (Series B) for $1000 maturing in 30 years, issued on 1 July 1915 by The Kansas City Railways Co., a corporation formed in 1914 in the state of Missouri. This bond, engraved by the American Banknote Co., New York, constituted part of an issue of $1 million. The company, which was reorganised in 1925, paid the interest on the coupons until 1935 and eventually passed into receivership.

Kansas City, St. Louis and Chicago Railroad Co.

Registered certificate for one share of $100 in the capital stock of the Kansas City, St. Louis and Chicago Railroad Co., dated 26 February 1914. The vignette on this share certificate, printed by the Western Banknote and Engraving Co., Chicago, is the same as that on the certificate of the Cincinnati, Wabash and Michigan Railway Co., also engraved by the same firm.

The company was formed in the state of Missouri in 1877 to extend the line of the Louisiana and Missouri River Railroad to Kansas City. In 1879, the same year as the extension was opened, the railway was leased in perpetuity to the Chicago and Alton Railroad Co. for 35 per cent of gross earnings, less taxes. The company was reorganised in 1947.

Kentucky and Great Eastern Railway Co.

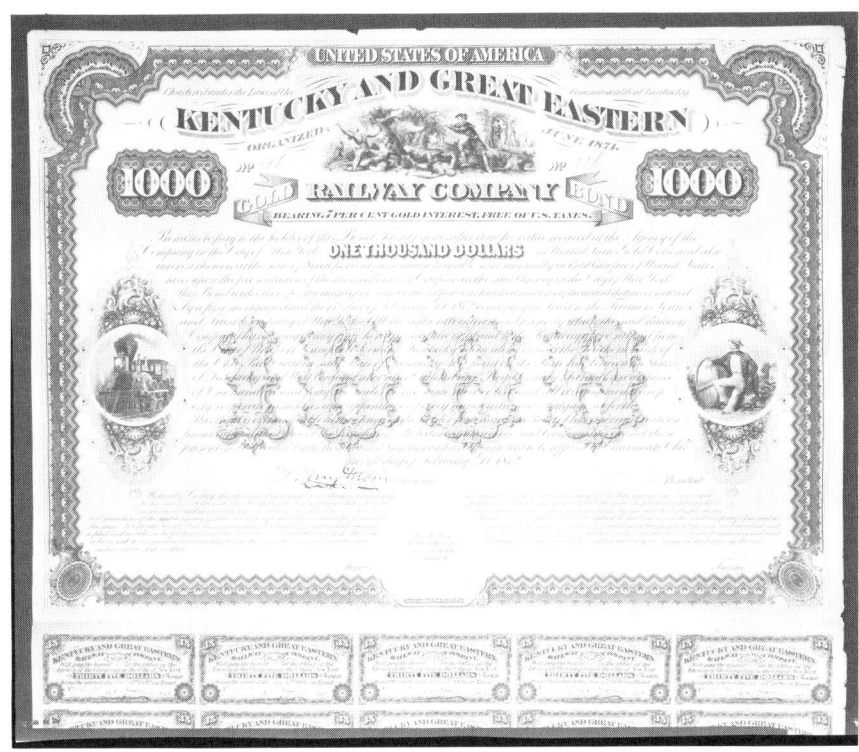

Unissued 20 year, seven per cent first mortgage gold bond to bearer for $1000 of the Kentucky and Great Eastern Railway Co. Secured by a first mortgage on the railway's franchises and property held over a stretch of 146 miles along the Ohio River to the border with West Virginia, the authorized loan totalled $2,190,000 and was dated 15 February 1872. However, no bonds were issued until 1875.

The remarkable vignette on the bond, printed by the American Banknote Co., was taken from an earlier plate engraved in 1858 by Rawdon, Wright, Hatch and Edson Co., a founder member of the American Banknote Co. It depicts Daniel Boone, the pioneer, saved from a band of Red Indians by his friend Simon Kenton who fired a musket shot into the heart of the assailant about to scalp Boone. The scene could be dated between 1775 and 1778 when Kenton became Daniel Boone's associate in helping to guide new settlers to Kentucky.

The company, which was formed in Kentucky in 1871 as successor to two railways sold under foreclosure, aimed at establishing a link between the coal and iron mines in eastern Kentucky and West Virginia and the existing railway network converging on Cincinnati. In 1875 its name was changed to the Kentucky Central Railroad Co.

(This certificate is illustrated in colour—Plate 3.)

Keokuk and Des Moines Railway Co.

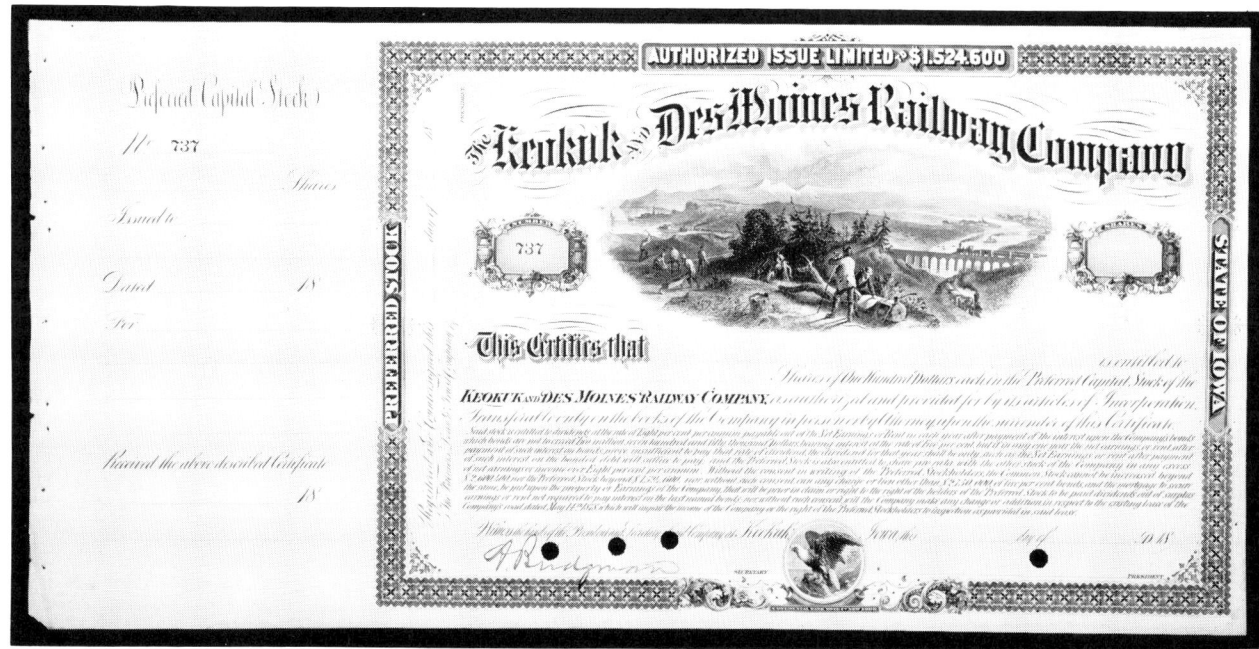

Unissued share certificate in the preferred capital stock of the Keokuk and Des Moines Railway Co., signed by the Secretary A. Bridgeman. The vignette on this certificate shows the full-scale picture of the engraving which appears in identical but restricted form on the unissued share certificate of the Fort Wayne, Cincinnati and Louisville Railroad Co., illustrated earlier. The Keokuk and Des Moines certificate was printed by the Continental Banknote Co., New York, a firm of printers and engravers which became affiliated to the American Banknote Co.

The company, which operated a line opened since 1870 had been formed in 1874, with an authorized capital of $1,524,000 preferred stock and $2,400,000 common stock, as a reorganisation of the eastern division of the Des Moines Valley Railroad which was sold under foreclosure in 1873. In 1878, the Keokuk and Des Moines Railway passed into the possession of the Chicago, Rock Island and Pacific Railroad Co. which leased it for 45 years.

(This certificate is illustrated in colour—Plate 4.)

Town of Hannibal: Lake Ontario Shore Rail Road Co. Municipal Bond.

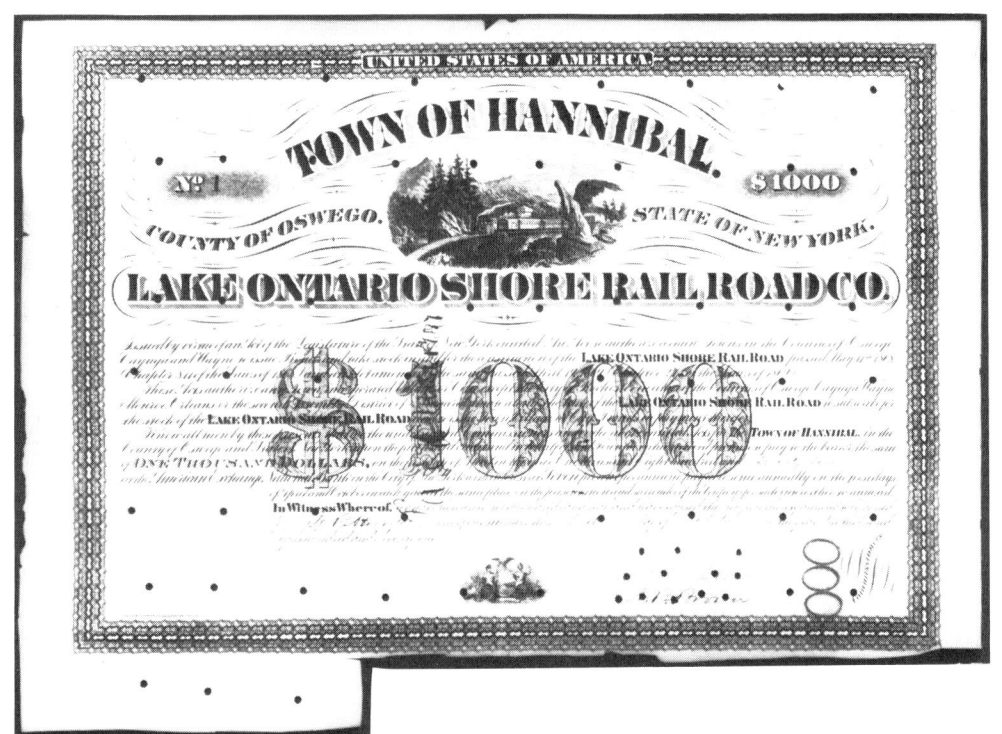

Seven per cent bond to bearer for $1000 of the Lake Ontario Shore Rail Road Co., dated 1 October 1871 for redemption on 1 April 1877.

Two months following the company's incorporation in March 1868, the legislature of the state of New York authorized certain towns situated along the proposed route of the railway to subscribe for the stock of the company and to issue town bonds by way of payment in order to finance the construction of the railway which opened to Ontario in 1873. The bond reproduced here, printed by Charles M. Cornwell, 247 Pearl St., New York, bears the serial number 1. It was issued by the Commissioners for the Town of Hannibal in County Oswego (New York).

Sold by foreclosure in September 1874, the company was reorganised under the title of Lake Ontario Railroad and became incorporated with the Rome, Watertown and Ogdenburgh Railroad.

Lehigh Valley Railroad Co.

Registered certificate for 100 shares of $50 each in the capital stock of the Lehigh Valley Railroad Co., dated 11 February 1892. The certificate, printed by the New York Banknote Co., shows on the vignette a portrait of Asa Packer, the railway's founding father.

Chartered under the title Lehigh Valley Railroad Co. by the state of Pennsylvania in January 1853, the company completed the construction of its main line in 1855. During the 1860s, it absorbed a number of smaller adjoining railways. Later it acquired a controlling interest in the Pennsylvania and New York Railroad. Operating as it did in the rich coal mining region of Pennsylvania, the Lehigh Valley Railroad derived most of its freight earnings from carrying coal, including anthracite. In 1896, the company introduced a new, luxurious and fast passenger train service between Jersey City and Buffalo, which was named the *Black Diamond Express* to commemorate its long and close association with the coal industry.

Louisiana and Missouri River Railroad Co.

Unissued certificate for 100 shares of $100 each of the Louisiana and Missouri River Railroad Co., signed by the President R. P. Tansey, and the Secretary. The certificate was printed by the American Banknote Co., New York.

The company, chartered by the state of Missouri in March 1868, was leased in perpetuity from August 1870 to the Chicago and Alton Railroad Co. at a rental of 35 per cent of gross earnings. The total projected line of railway was to extend from Louisiana to Kansas City. The first section opened in 1871.

Louisville Railway Co.

Registered certificate for 10 shares of $100 each in the common stock of the Louisville Railway Co., dated 14 December 1893. The certificate, with its vignette of an allegorical figure of electricity and one of the company's tramways, was printed by the American Banknote Co., Philadelphia. The same design is also used on the certificate of the Trenton Street Railway Co. of 1899.

The company was formed in Kentucky in 1890 with a share capital of $6 million, consisting of $5 million common stock and $1 million preferred. It operated an electric city and suburban tramway. On 4 April 1893, the structure of the share capital was modified by the company, increasing the preferred stock to $2 million while the common stock was reduced to $4 million.

Boston, Hartford and Erie Rail Road Co.

Plate 1

Cleveland, Columbus, Cincinnati & Indianapolis Railway

Plate 2

Kentucky and Great Eastern Railway Co.

Plate 3

Keokuk and Des Moines Railway Co.

Plate 4

Missouri, Kansas and Texas Railway Co.

Plate 5

New York, Pennsylvania and Ohio Rail-Road Co.

Plate 7 — *Plymouth, Kankakee and Pacific Railroad Co.*

South Mountain Railroad Co.

Plate 8

Marquette, Houghton and Ontonagon Railroad Co.

Unissued share certificate of the Marquette, Houghton and Ontonagon Railroad Co., printed by The Homer Lee Banknote Co., New York.

Organised in the state of Michigan in 1872, the company, which counted John J. Astor among its directors, operated a network of some 88 miles, with branches to a number of mines in north eastern Michigan. On 16 April 1883, it was consolidated with the Houghton and L'Anse Railroad Co. A new consolidated company was formed with an increased share capital following the absorption of the Houghton and L'Anse Railroad Co. which extended the total length of lines in the system. The certificate illustrated here is one from the new consolidated company.

Michigan Central Railroad Co.

Unissued 3½ per cent gold bond for $5000 for redemption on 1 May 1952 of the Michigan Central Railroad Co., incorporated by the state of Michigan. This bond, one of an issue of $18 million, was secured by a first mortgage dated 1 May 1902 covering the main line of the railway and by a supplementary mortgage dated 1 January 1903. The certificate was printed by the American Banknote Co., New York.

Minneapolis, St. Paul and Sault Ste. Marie Railway Co.

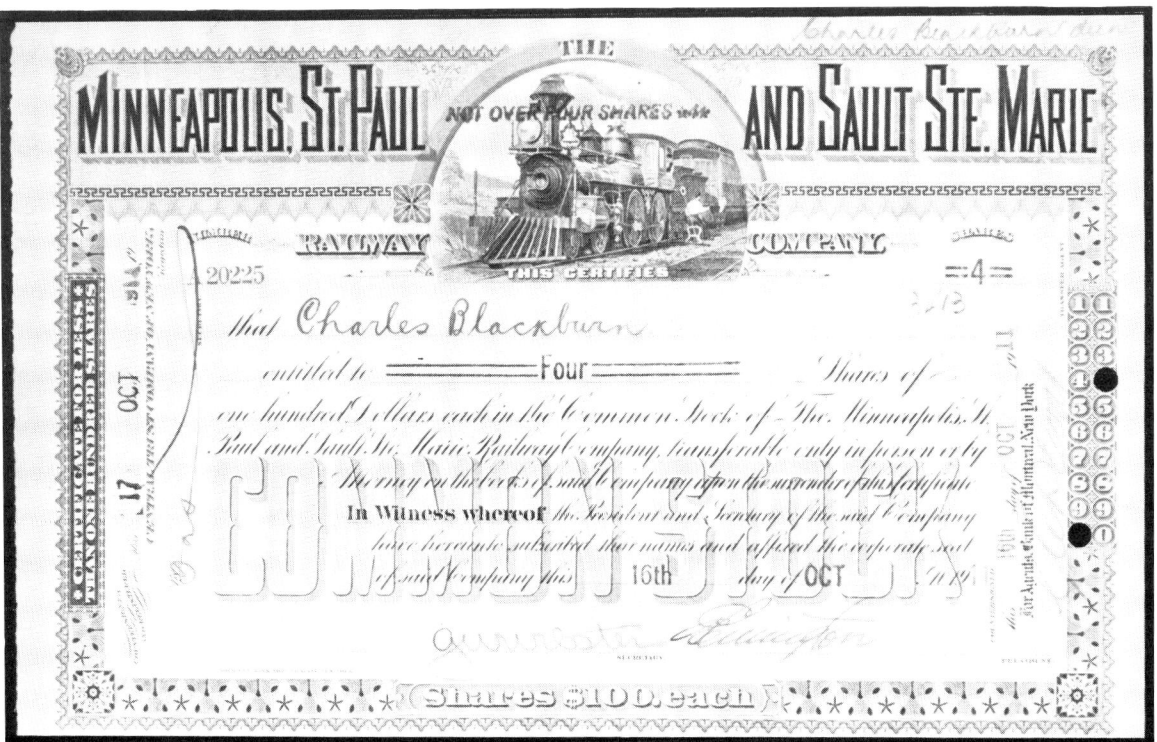

Registered certificate for four shares of $100 each in the preferred capital stock of the Minneapolis, St. Paul and Sault Ste. Marie Railway Co., dated 16 October 1911. The certificate was printed by the American Banknote Co., New York.

The company, chartered in 1883 to build a railway from Minneapolis and St. Paul to Sault Ste. Marie, was entitled Minneapolis, Sault Ste. Marie and Atlantic Railway. It was intended as a connection between the Northern Pacific Railroad Co. in Minneapolis and the Canadian Pacific at Sault Ste. Marie.

Missouri, Kansas and Texas Railway Co.

Registered certificate for 100 shares of $100 each of the Missouri, Kansas and Texas Railway Co., dated 8 April 1880 and signed by Jay Gould as president. The company was organised in 1870 by the consolidation of four south-western railways. Despite its strategic position and large volume of business, the declining company, falling a victim to depression, was staggering from one financial crisis to the next. After a short period under receivership in the late 1870s, the railway's property was placed in the hands of a trust company in the interest of its bondholders. Still heavily in debt in 1879, the Missouri, Kansas and Texas was acquired by Jay Gould, who, in the struggle for control, outwitted another interested party, the Chicago, Burlington and Quincy Railroad Co. In October 1879, a few days after the bondholders rejected the Burlington's offer, the price of the Missouri, Kansas and Texas rose sharply in one day from $22 to $25, and on the next day to $29. The *New York Tribune* remarked that 'it would require a very powerful microscope to discover one tenth of that price in the present value of that stock'. Gould's connection with the buying was as yet not suspected. By purchasing at the going market prices, which a conservative railway management would have considered too high, Gould achieved his aim to acquire a majority shareholding. Losing no time with his new conquest, he reshuffled the board of directors in January 1880, and installed men of his own choice, with himself as president. By May 1880, he had persuaded the shareholders to approve a lease of the railway to the Missouri Pacific. Aware that the latter's control would be ineffective as long as the Missouri, Kansas and Texas bondholders could challenge any decision, Gould took steps to make the trust company return the railway property to the shareholders by fully honouring the unpaid interest on the bonds. In October 1880, a court order demanded restoration of the company to the shareholders. Gould's victory was complete and the Missouri Pacific was in control of the Missouri, Kansas and Texas whose business could be diverted at will to other Gould lines.

(This certificate is illustrated in colour—Plate 5.)

Missouri, Kansas and Texas Railway Co.

Registered certificate for 100 shares of $100 each of the preferred stock of the Missouri, Kansas and Texas Railway Co., dated 27 January 1892. By that time, Jay Gould's era was over; in 1889, the control that he held on the company was slipping. The reorganisation, which took place in 1890, brought a dramatic change to the company. With the election as president of Harry K. Enos, a representative of Rockefeller's Standard Oil, the Missouri, Kansas and Texas was lost to Gould. At the next annual meeting in the spring of 1891, John D. Rockefeller, who was one of the largest shareholders of the company, became a member of the board, which was from then on controlled by the Rockefeller interests.

The vignettes on this share of the reorganised company show an engine stoker in action and a train waiting at a station. The certificate was printed by Franklin Banknote Co., New York.

Missouri, Kansas & Texas Railway Co.

Another example of a share of the Missouri, Kansas & Texas Railway Co., this registered certificate for 10 shares of $100 in the common stock is dated 23 May 1895. It bears a two-shilling embossed British revenue stamp. The vignette on the certificate, also printed by the Franklin Banknote Co., New York, depicts an engine roundhouse.

Missouri-Kansas-Texas Railroad Co.

Registered certificate for 75 preferred shares of the Missouri-Kansas-Texas Railroad Co., dated 21 April 1923. The certificate, printed by the American Banknote Co., shows an express passing through a station, while a party of surveyors are seen working on the left.

This company was formed in 1922 in the state of Missouri as successor to the Missouri, Kansas & Texas Railway Co. which was placed in the hands of a receiver in September 1915 and sold under foreclosure in 1923. In the early part of the twentieth century, the Missouri, Kansas & Texas had rapidly expanded through several mergers and takeovers. Among others, it had purchased in June 1910 practically all the stock of The Texas Central Railroad, and in 1911 acquired control of the Wichita Falls & Northwestern Railway. In the reorganisation plan which was drawn up after the failure of the company, a new corporation, the Missouri-Kansas-Texas Railroad was formed on 6 July 1922 and registered under the laws of the state of Missouri with a 1000 year charter. The company owned an extensive network of lines which radiated mainly south and southwest of Kansas City, ramifying through the states of Kansas, Oklahoma and Texas. The company traditionally derived its major freight income from the transport of wheat.

Mobile and Ohio Rail Road Co.

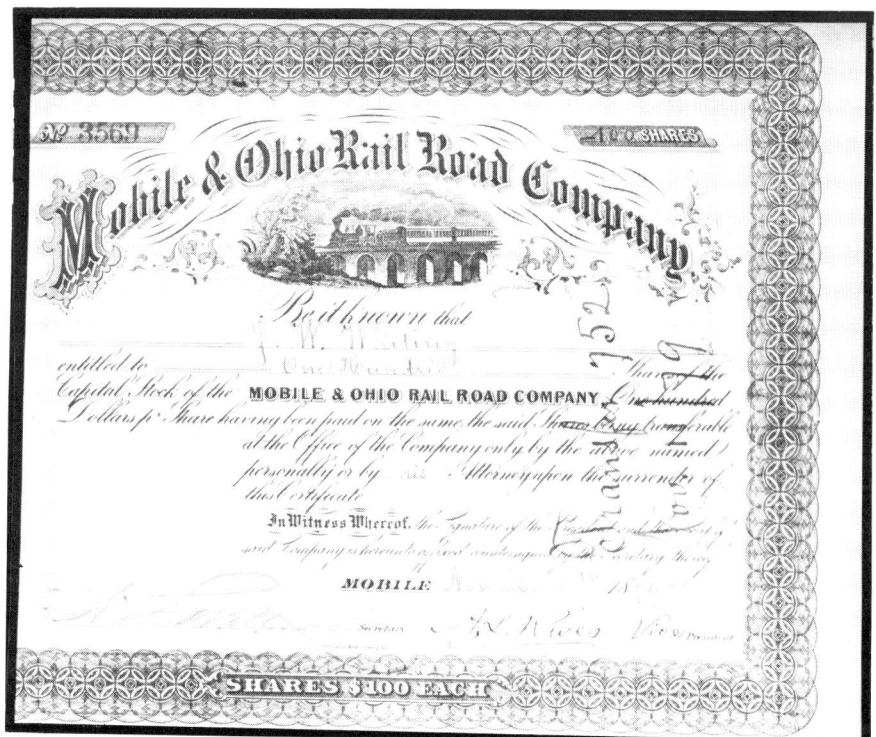

Registered certificate for 100 shares of $100 each of the Mobile and Ohio Rail Road Co., dated 4 November 1879. This certificate is signed by the company's Vice President, A. L. Rives who had been promoted from his former position as general manager, and by the Secretary, Alonzo L. Willoughby who also acted as Treasurer.

Chartered on 8 February 1848 in Alabama and later in the states of Mississipi, Tennessee and Kentucky, the company opened its main line from Mobile to Columbus in 1861. In 1850 it had received the first land grant authorized by Congress for railway purposes. In 1875, the company having defaulted on payment of interest, a receiver took over the railway and its property, which were restored to the company without a sale in 1883 as its indebtedness was funded into several morgage loans secured on the land held.

Muscatine, Western Railway Construction Co.

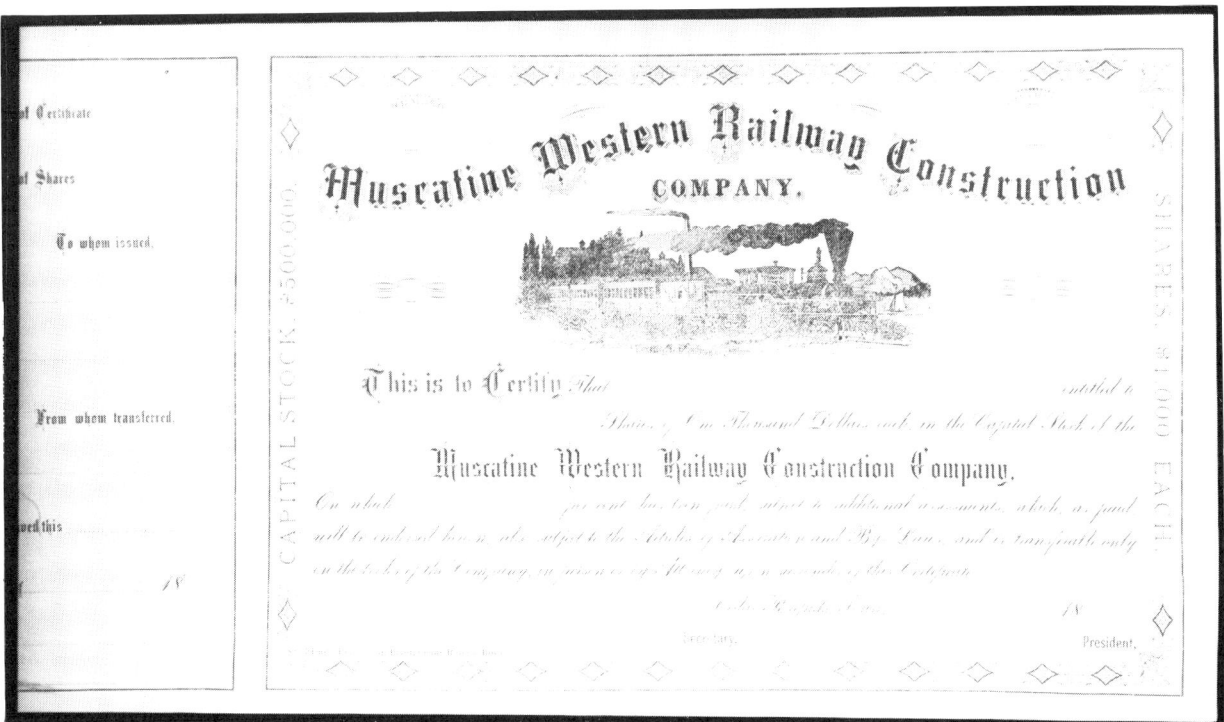

Unissued partly-paid certificate of the Muscatine, Western Railway Construction Co., which had been formed in the state of Iowa for the specific purpose of building a railway. Its share capital totalled $500,000 divided into shares of the unusually high value of $1000. This partly-paid certificate printed by the Daily Republican Print, Cedar Rapids, Iowa, was to be issued to subscribers having paid an initial deposit on the stock. The shareholders were liable for further calls at the company's discretion, until the shares became fully paid.

New Haven, Middletown and Willimantic Rail Road Co.

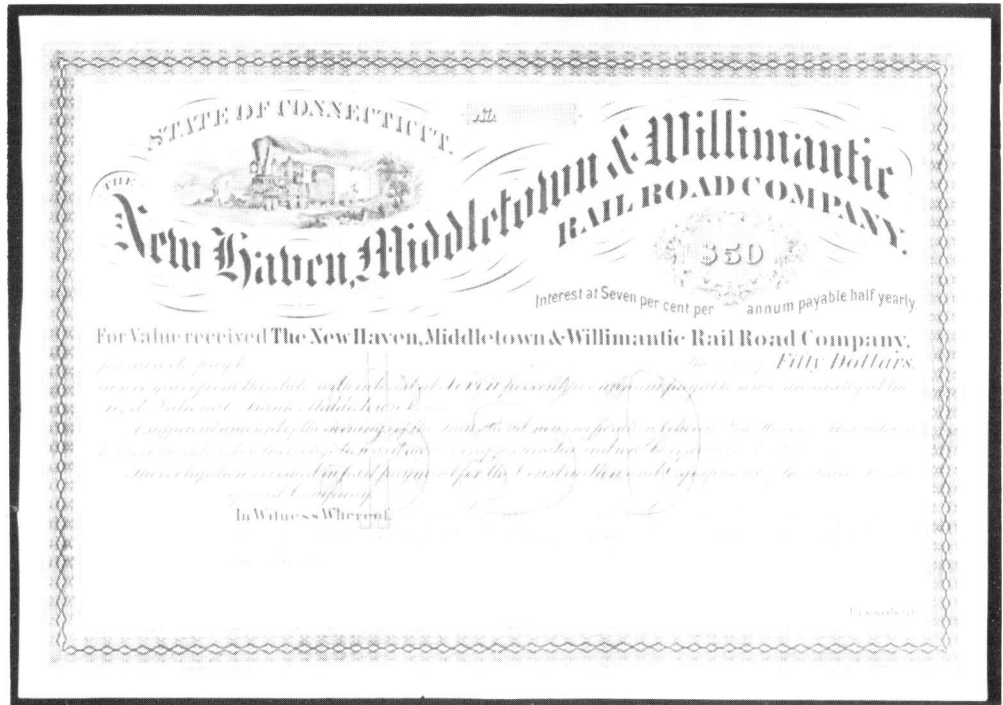

Unissued five year seven per cent bond for $50 of the New Haven, Middletown and Willimantic Rail Road Co., dated 1870. The company's earnings on the section of the railway already in operation between New Haven and Middletown in Connecticut were to meet the interest payments on these bonds which were issued in part payment for the construction and equipment of the railway. The certificate was printed by Maverick, Stephan and Co., 176 Fulton St., New York.

The railway company, originally chartered in 1846 in Connecticut as the New York and Boston Railroad, was re-incorporated under the title of New Haven, Middletown and Willimantic Railroad Co. in 1867. The remainder of the line was completed to Willimantic in 1873. Following its sale under foreclosure of the mortgage in 1875, the company was re-chartered in the plan of reorganisation as the Boston and New York Air Line Railroad Co., the bonds of the New Haven, Middletown and Willimantic Railroad Co. having been exchanged for the new stock.

New Orleans Great Northern Railroad Co.

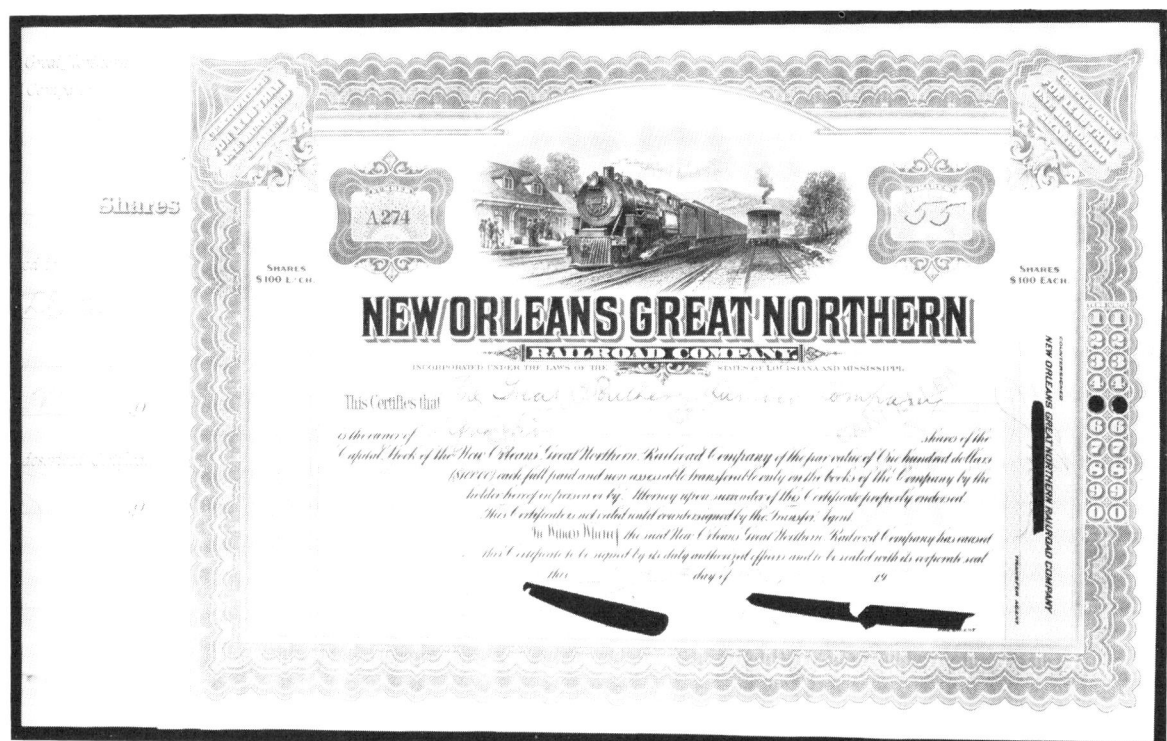

Registered certificate for 55 shares of $100 each of the New Orleans Great Northern Railroad Co., dated 27 December 1913. The share certificate of this company, incorporated in the states of Louisiana and Mississipi in 1905, was printed by the American Banknote Co., New York.

New Orleans Great Northern Railway Co.

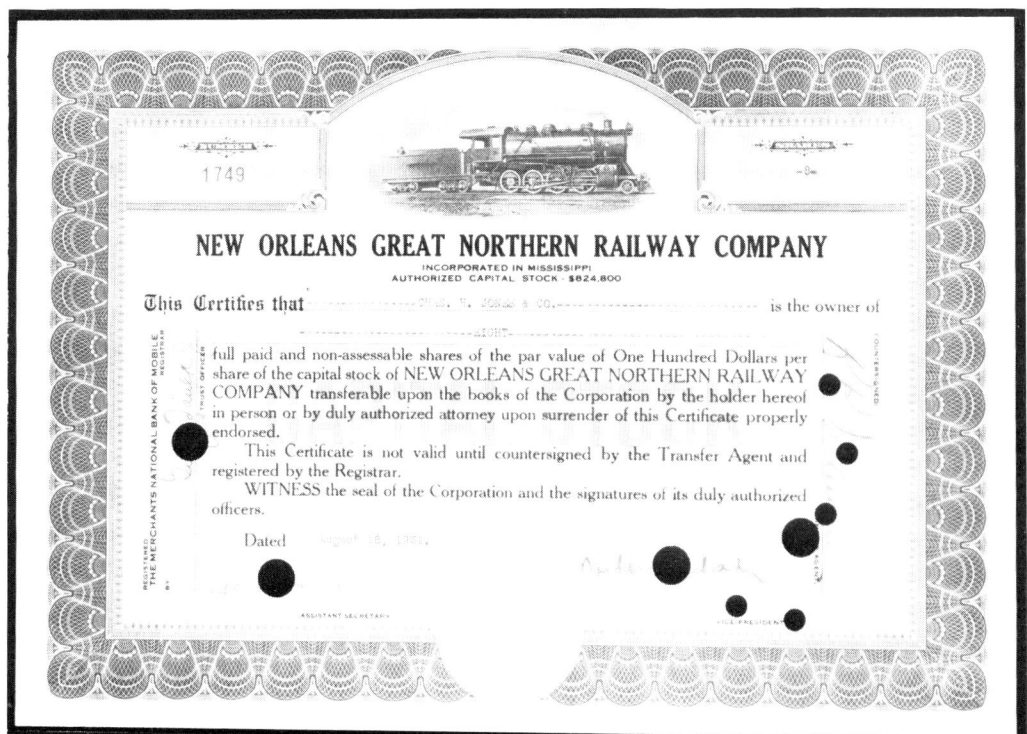

Registered certificate for eight shares of $100 each of the New Orleans Great Northern Railway Co., dated 18 August 1934. This certificate was printed by the Security Banknote Co., Philadelphia.

The railway company was incorporated in the state of Mississipi in 1933, as successor to the New Orleans Great Northern Railroad Co.

New Orleans, Mobile and Chicago Railroad Co.

Registered certificate for one share in the preferred stock of the New Orleans Mobile and Chicago Railroad Co., dated 1 July 1910. The certificate was printed by the American Banknote Co., New York.

The company was chartered in the states of Alabama, Mississipi and Tennessee in 1909 with a share capital consisting of $5 million preferred shares and $11,500,000 common shares. In 1915 the bonds issued by the company had to be foreclosed.

The New York, Chicago and St. Louis Railroad Co.

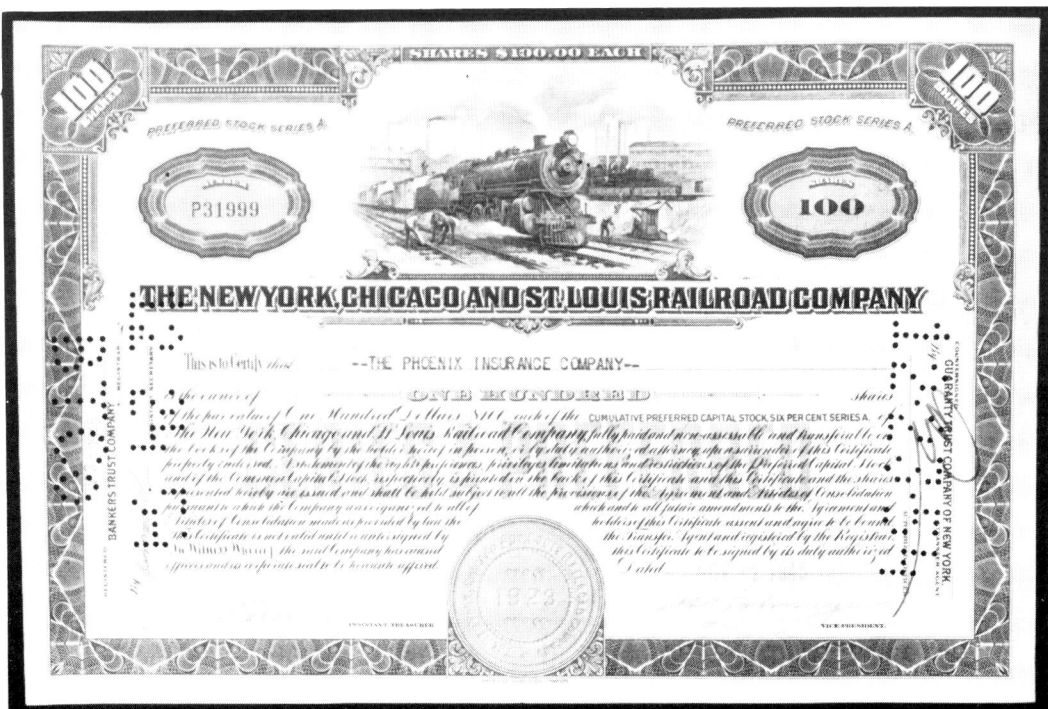

Registered certificate for 100 shares of $100 of the cumulative preferred stock (series A) of the New York, Chicago and St. Louis Railroad Co., dated 23 June 1944. The American Banknote Co. printed the certificate of this company which was formed in 1923.

New York and Fort Lee Rail Road Co.

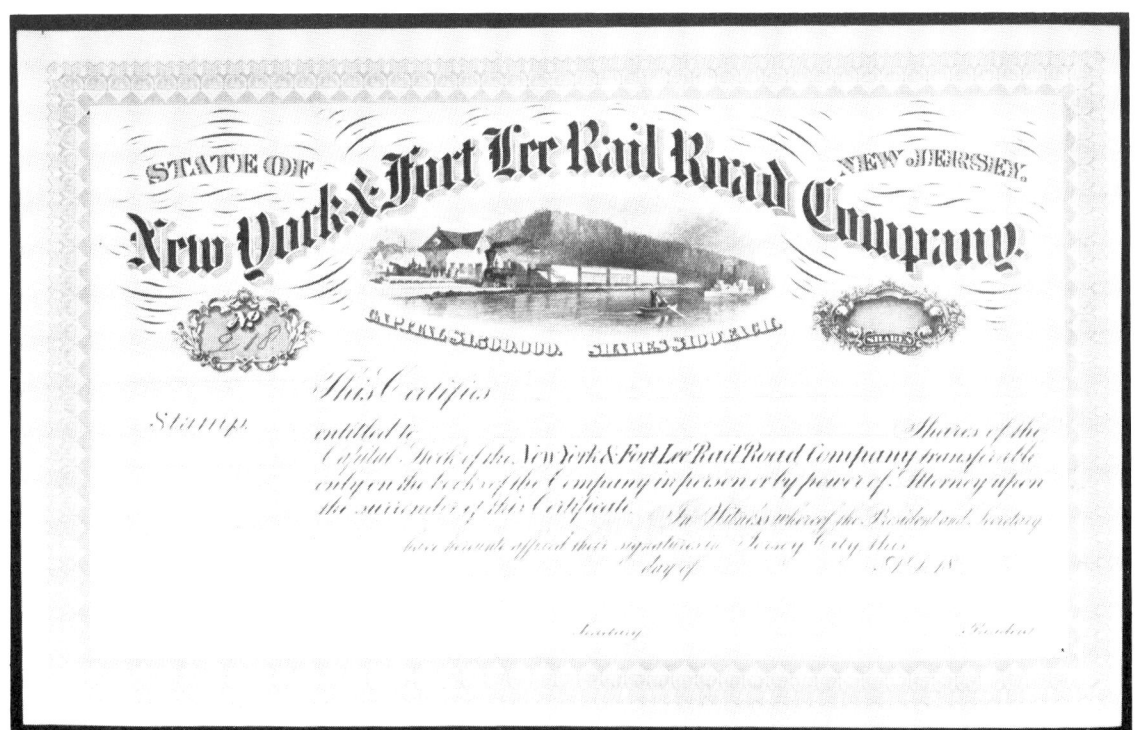

Unissued share certificate of the New York and Fort Lee Rail Road Co. which was formed in the state of New Jersey with a capital of $1,500,000 divided into shares of $100. From December 1868, the Erie Railway leased the railway at a rental of one cent per ton per mile.

The New York and Harlem Rail Road Co.

Registered certificate for 100 shares of $50 each of the New York and Harlem Rail Road Co., dated 6 June 1870.

The New York and Harlem Railroad Co. had been chartered in April 1831. In 1852 the railway ran from New York to Chatham, where it connected with another for Buffalo. In the late 1850s when Cornelius Vanderbilt switched from steamers to railways, one of the first two railways acquired by the old Commodore, then well into his sixties and already a very rich man, was the New York and Harlem Railroad Co. During 1862-1863 he bought control of it at $9 a share at a time when the railway and equipment were badly run down. Shortly after the acquisition, the share price shot up. Vanderbilt had obtained a new franchise to extend the railway's right of way by bribing the Council. In a conspiracy with members of the Council to revoke the franchise, Vanderbilt's competitors George Law (of the Hudson River Railroad, which later became a Vanderbilt line and was amalgamated with the New York Central system), and Daniel Drew formed a pool to sell the New York and Harlem shares short. Despite Drew's heavy selling, the shares which had shot up to $100 stayed firm. In fact Vanderbilt who had got wind of the plot was himself buying all the shares sold by Drew until he owned practically all the 110,000 shares of the company. He then called on Drew to make delivery, knowing full well that there was no stock to buy as he owned it all. Drew was forced to buy from Vanderbilt thousands of shares at $179 which came close to the amount Vanderbilt had paid for the control of the company. However, he lost the new franchise. His son, William H. Vanderbilt, whose signature as Third Vice-President of the company appears at the bottom of this certificate, inherited most of his father's fortune after the Commodore's death in January 1877, having won his respect in successfully managing the Vanderbilt railway properties.

New York and New England Railroad Co.

Six per cent second mortgage bond to bearer for $1000, issued on 1 August 1882 by the New York and New England Railroad Co. for redemption in 1902. The certificate was printed by the American Banknote Co., New York and Boston.

The company was formed in 1873 by the holders of the 'Berdell' mortgage bonds issued by the former Boston, Hartford and Erie Railroad Co. The latter company, created in 1863, had undertaken to construct a new railway line from Boston to the Hudson River, which it intended to finance by floating the 'Berdell' bonds to the amount of $20 million. However, the total issue only just paid for the already existing debts of the railway company and for a portion of some 100 miles of new line. Having defaulted on the payment of interest on its bonds, the Boston, Hartford and Erie Railroad Co. entered into liquidation. A new company entitled the New York and New England Railroad Co. was organised, with holders of the $20 million 'Berdell' bonds becoming shareholders to equal amounts in the new company. To pay off the remaining debts and complete the line, the New York and New England Railroad Co. issued in 1882 the six per cent mortgage bonds to the amount of $10 million, of which there were 5000 bonds of $1000.

New York and New England Railroad Co.

Registered certificate for 100 shares of $100 in the capital stock of the New York and New England Railroad Co., dated 15 October 1886. At the beginning of that year, the company successfully emerged from a difficult period when it had been threatened by receivership after failing in 1884 to pay its fixed charges and to provide for its floating debt. This certificate, printed by the Continental Banknote Co., New York, was signed by the President Charles P. Clark and the Treasurer, George B. Phippen, who held the same position in 1882 (see mortgage bond).

New York and New Haven Rail Road Co.

Unissued six per cent mortgage bond to bearer for $1000 of the New York and New Haven Rail Road Co., which had been chartered in Connecticut on 20 June 1844. This bond, dated 1865 for redemption in 1885, formed part of a total issue of $3 million. On 24 July 1872, the company was merged into the New York, New Haven & Hartford Railroad Co. This certificate was printed by E. B. Claytons & Sons, 157 Pearl St., New York.

The New York, New Haven and Hartford Railroad Co.

Registered debenture of March 1897 for $10,000, yielding four per cent and maturing in 1947, issued on 19 February 1898 by The New York, New Haven and Hartford Railroad Co. The certificate was printed by the American Banknote Co., New York.

This company had been formed in 1872 as a consolidation of the New York and New Haven Railroad and the Hartford and New Haven Railroad companies, both chartered much earlier. In 1882, it leased the Boston & New York Air Line Railroad and obtained a controlling interest in the Hartford and Connecticut Valley Railroad. With the approval of the shareholders, the company's charter was amended in 1881 to allow it to acquire and use steamers and ferries, as well as to buy and sell shares in any Connecticut company owning or operating ferryboats, providing the expenditure did not exceed two per cent of the company's stock.

The New York, New Haven and Hartford Railroad Co.

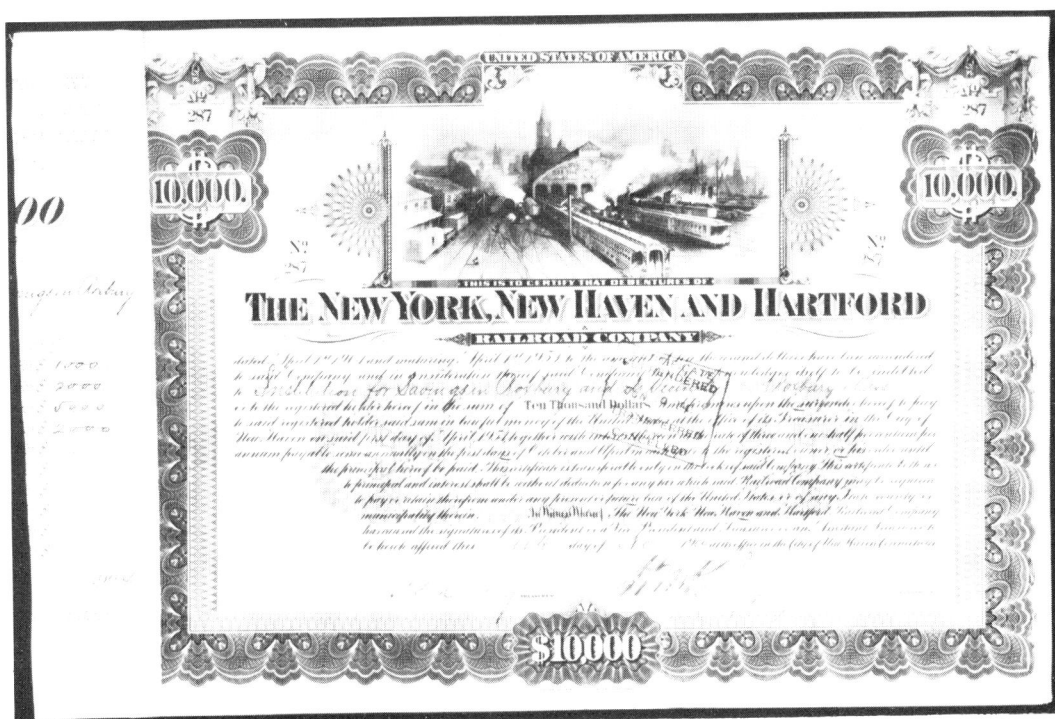

This fifty-year 3½ per cent registered debenture for $10,000 was issued on 11 November 1904 by the New York, New Haven and Hartford Railroad Co. More recent than the preceding one, this certificate, also engraved by the American Banknote Co. New York, shows a different vignette with trains in a station. It was cancelled in 1941 because the registered holders converted the debenture into bearer bonds.

Towards the end of the first decade of the twentieth century, the New York, New Haven & Hartford Railroad, which J. P. Morgan had organised over the years into an elaborate system of railways, steamers and tramways at very great cost, was approaching bankruptcy, throwing thousands of small shareholders into ruin. The scandal took such large proportions that the affairs of the company over the last ten years were subjected to a thorough investigation which disclosed numerous instances of gross maladministration and illegal practices, and compelled Morgan, then 76 years old, to give evidence on the witness stand in December 1912.

The New York, New Haven and Hartford Railroad Co.

Fifty year 3½ per cent registered convertible debenture for $5000, issued on 19 September 1906 by the New York, New Haven & Hartford Railroad Co. These debentures could be converted into shares of the company between 1911 and 1916, which is the reason for the cancellation of this certificate, exchanged for stock. The vignette on this certificate is identical to that of the Rock Island Co. of 1914, both of which were engraved by the American Banknote Co.

In the ten years from 1903, the company's capitalisation had increased from $93 million to $417 million. The debenture illustrated here, which formed part of a total issue of $30 million, is an example of one among several similar capital increases during that period. Of this increase in the share capital, roughly $120 million were truly devoted to the railway and spent on improvements and new equipment, but over $200 million went on financing operations completely outside the railway sphere. The company practically monopolised the freight and passenger business in five states, as well as steamship lines and trolleys in the areas also served by the railway. In its investigation of 1914, the Interstate Commerce Commission scathingly reported that 'the financial operations necessary for these acquisitions and the losses which they have entailed, have been skillfully concealed by the juggling of money and securities from one subsidiary corporation to another'. This critical comment was particularly aimed at J. P. Morgan, in his position as banker as well as director of this railway company.

The New York, New Haven and Hartford Railroad Co.

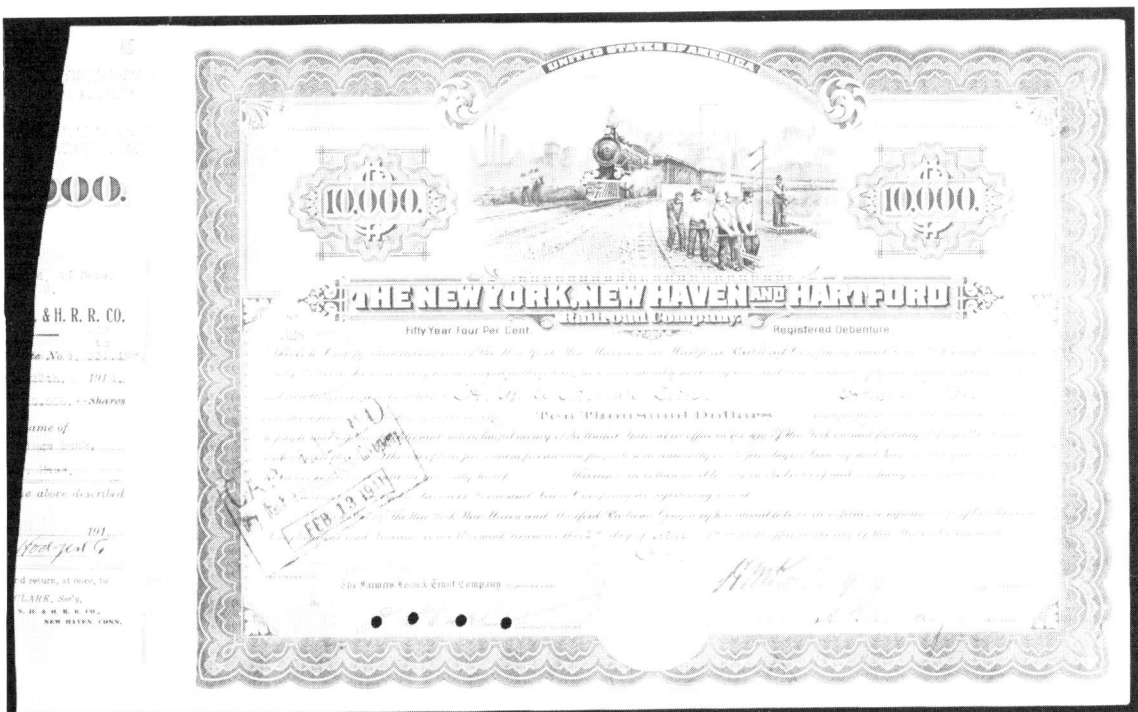

Fifty year four per cent registered debenture for $10,000, issued on 27 January 1914 by the New York New Haven and Hartford Railroad Co. This certificate, also printed by the American Banknote Co., depicts a steam train travelling past a group of labourers replacing a section of rail.

Despite the Interstate Commerce Commission's grim findings in its report of 1914, the New York, New Haven & Hartford Railroad was allowed to survive although the shares had sunk to practically nothing and paid no dividends for 10 years. The investigation, which blamed J. P. Morgan for his dominating influence on the company's affairs, had revealed grossly exaggerated prices paid for various railway acquisitions, large sums spent on influencing public opinion through the press, fictitious sales of the company's shares to 'friendly parties' to inflate the share price and payments of money to politicians and legislators.

The New York, New Haven and Hartford Railroad Co.

Four per cent registered 50 year gold debenture for $10,000 of 1907, issued by the New York, New Haven and Hartford Railroad Co. on 1 May 1920. This certificate, depicting an engraving by the American Banknote Co. of an electrified line, formed part of a total issue of $16,758,000.

New York and Northern Railway Co.

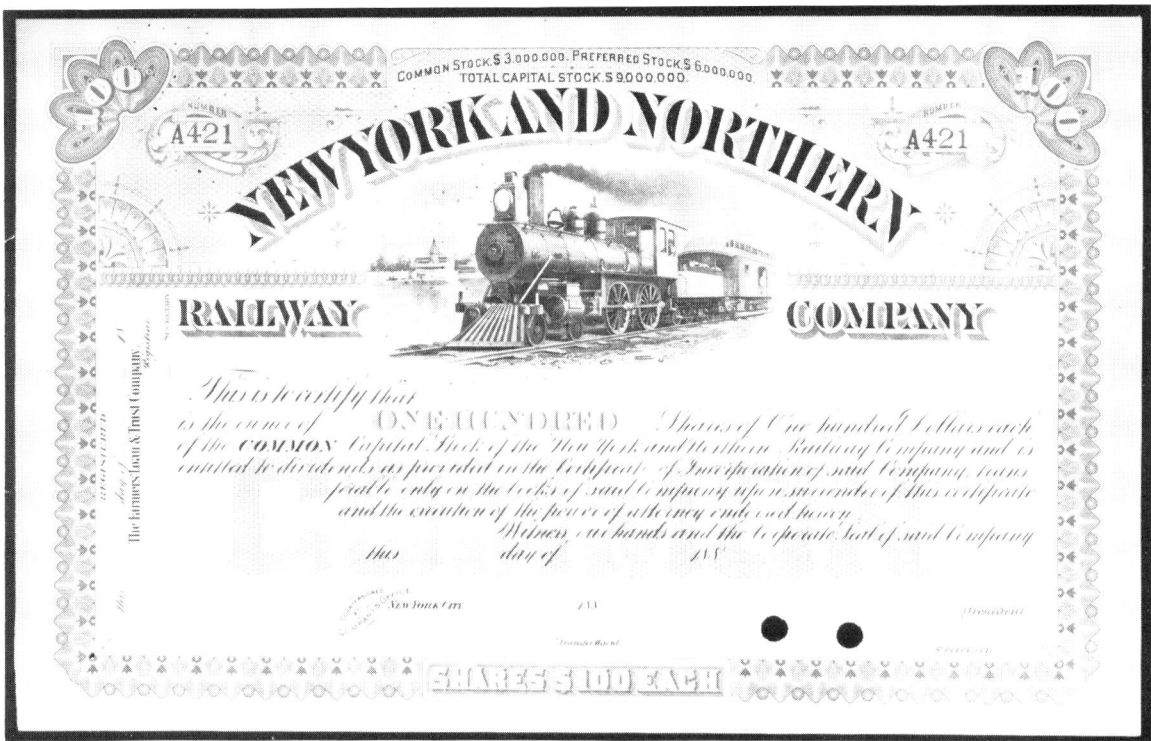

Unissued certificate for 100 shares of $100 each in the common capital stock of the New York and Northern Railway Co.

Formed on 11 October 1887 in the state of New York with a share capital of $9 million, this company existed until December 1893 when it was wound up by foreclosure. It was reorganised in January 1894 as the New York and Putnam Railroad Co.

New York, Ontario and Western Railway Co.

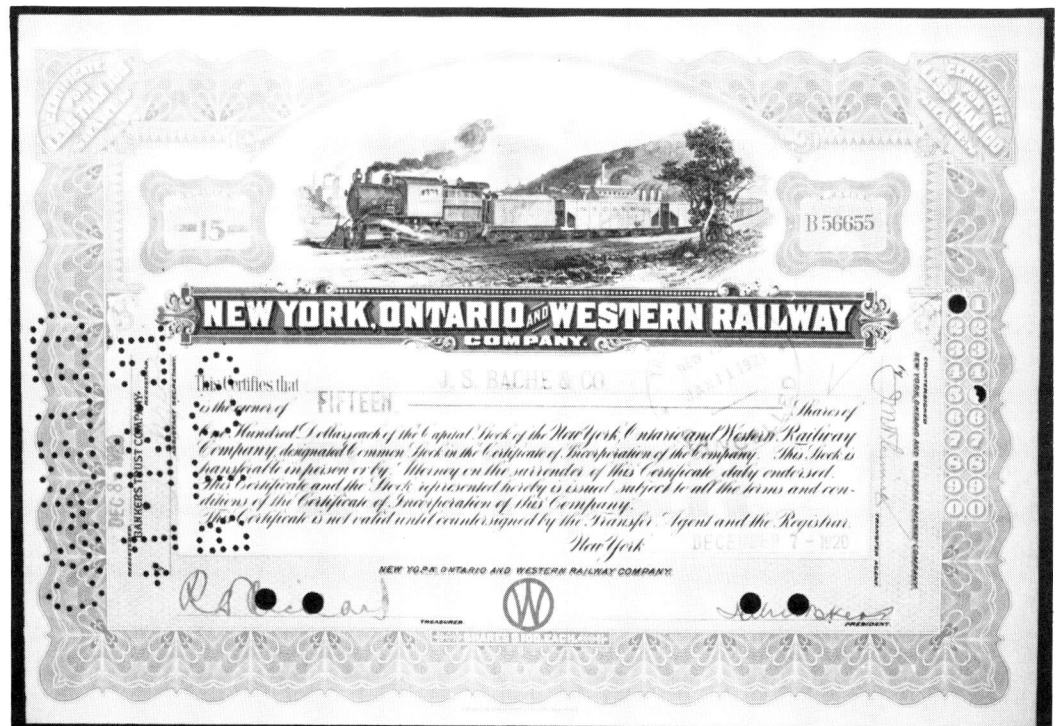

Registered certificate for 15 shares of $100 in the capital stock of the New York, Ontario & Western Railway Co., dated 7 December 1920. This certificate, engraved by the American Banknote Co., New York, shows an example of the 'camelback' engine, a type of steam locomotive developed in America during the 1880s where the driver's cab sits astride the boiler, thus giving it a distinctive 'hump' in the middle.

This company was formed as a reorganisation of the main line of the New York and Oswego Midland Railroad which was sold in November 1879 in the interest of its shareholders and creditors. The company was reorganised in 1937.

Town of Hastings New York and Oswego Midland Rail Road. Municipal Bond

Seven per cent bearer bond for $100 maturing in 1888 of the New York and Oswego Midland Rail Road, issued on 1 January 1868 by the town of Hastings, County Oswego (New York). Following an Act of 1867 passed by the legislature of the state of New York to facilitate the construction of a railway between New York and the lakes and to authorize towns along its route to subscribe to the company's shares, the town of Hastings issued a series of bonds in payment for the stock held in the company. This certificate, signed by the commissioners acting for the town of Hastings, bears the serial number 3. The New York & Oswego Midland Railroad, organised in January 1866, defaulted on the payment of interest on its bonds and passed into the hands of receivers in 1873. In 1879, its main line was organised as the New York, Ontario & Western Railway.

New York, Pennsylvania & Ohio Railroad Co.

Second mortgage 30 year five per cent gold bond to bearer for $500, or £100, issued by the New York, Pennsylvania & Ohio Railroad Co. on 7 May 1880. This certificate formed part of a series of bonds in denominations of $1000, or £200, and $500, or £100, amounting to a total of $14,500,000 (or £2,900,000) secured by a second mortgage on the railway's property and franchises. The company was incorporated in March 1880 as successor to the Atlantic & Great Western Railroad which was placed under receivership after being leased to the Erie Railway and sold under foreclosure in January 1880. Under the terms of the reorganisation which followed a few months later, first, second and third mortgage bonds were issued in addition to the common and preferred share capital which was held in trust by five voting trustees appointed by the bondholders, who thus retained a substantial control in the company.

This bond is signed by the President, J. H. Devereux, who had acted as receiver of the Atlantic & Great Western Railroad. The bonds of the first, second and third mortgages were listed on the London stock exchange. Printed by the Franklin Banknote Co., New York, this certificate bears a two-shilling British embossed revenue stamp.

New York, Pennsylvania & Ohio Railroad Co.

Registered non-voting beneficiary certificate for 50 shares of $50 each in the preferred capital stock of the New York, Pennsylvania and Ohio Railroad Co., dated 30 October 1885. The certificate was signed by the company secretary, Thos. Warnock and a representative of the trustees.

In the reorganisation of 1880, the company's share capital, constituted by 200,000 preferred shares of $50 and 700,000 common shares of $50, was held in trust by five voting trustees named by the mortgage bondholders.

(This certificate is illustrated in colour—Plate 6.)

New York, Providence & Boston Railroad Co.

Registered partly-paid certificate for 25 shares with a paid deposit of $35 per share in the capital stock of the New York, Providence & Boston Railroad Co., dated 12 January 1836. The certificate was engraved by Rawdon, Wright, Hatch & Co., New York.

Chartered in June 1832, the company opened the line from Providence (Rhode Island) to New London (Connecticut) in 1837.

Norfolk Southern Railroad Co.

Registered certificate for 100 shares of $100 each of the Norfolk Southern Railroad Co., dated 22 December 1936. The certificate was printed by the American Banknote Co., New York.

Chartered in Virginia as the Elizabeth City & Norfolk Railroad Co. in 1870, the company changed its name to the Norfolk Southern Railroad in February 1883. By 1936, the share capital stood at $16 million.

Old Colony and Newport Railway Co.

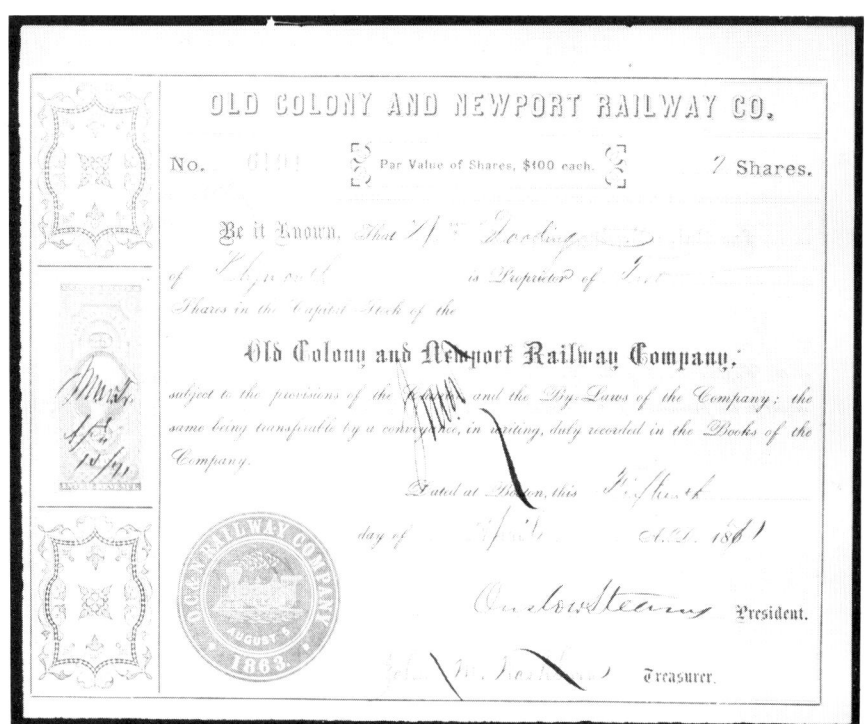

Registered certificate for two shares of $100 each in the capital stock of the Old Colony and Newport Railway Co., dated 15 April 1871. This certificate is signed by the President, Onslow Stearns and the Treasurer, John M. Washburn.

From an original charter of 1844, the Old Colony & Newport Railway Co. was incorporated in August 1863 as a consolidation with other railways. The line from Boston to Newport (Rhode Island) opened in 1864. In 1871 the rolling-stock of the company comprised 45 engines and 826 wagons operating over 303 miles of track.

Omaha and Council Bluffs Street Railway Co.

Registered certificate for 10 preferred shares of $100 each of the Omaha and Council Bluffs Street Railway Co., dated 6 August 1912. This certificate is engraved by the American Banknote Co., New York, with the same vignette as on the certificates on the Philadelphia Traction Co. of 1908 and the Utica and Mohawk Valley Railway Co.

Incorporated in the state of Nebraska the company, operating a city tramway, had an issued capital of $15 million, comprised of $5 million preferred and $10 million common shares. In 1955, it changed its name to Omaha Transit Co.

Penn Central Co.

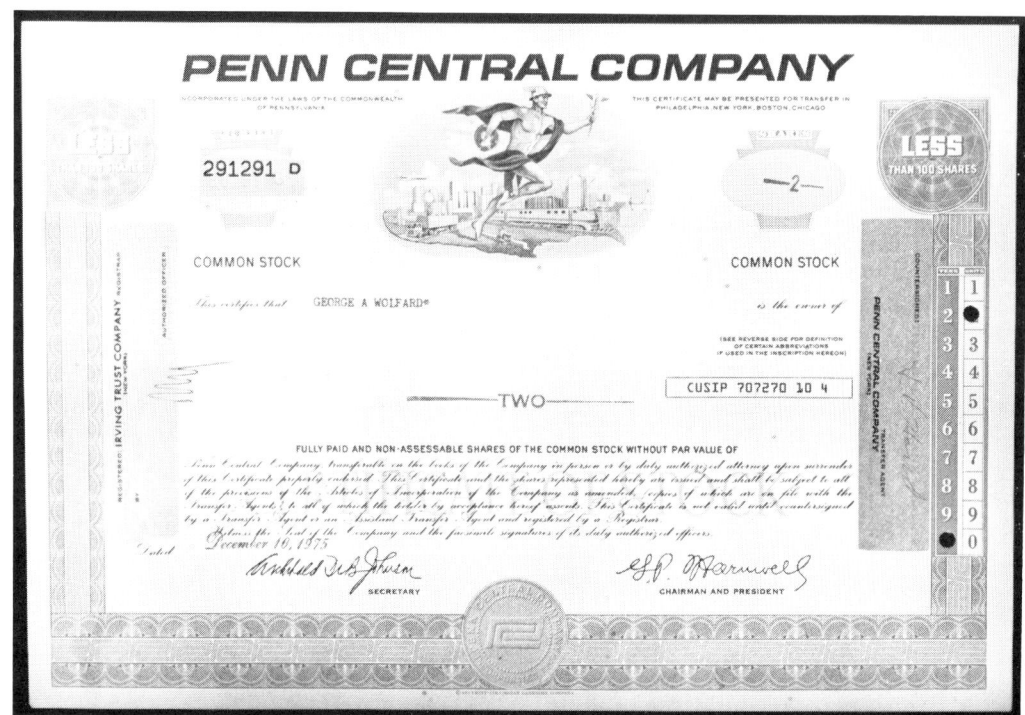

Registered certificate for two shares without par value of the Penn Central Co., dated 10 December 1975.

The Penn Central was the successor of the old Pennsylvania Railroad Co. chartered on 13 April 1846. The original line ran from Harrisburg to Pittsburgh. Over the years, the company acquired a great number of lines, building a vast railway network which extended throughout Pennsylvania and into the adjoining states. Electrification was introduced in 1925 on the line from New York to Washington and in 1957, the entire network was operated by diesel and electric power. In the merger with the New York Central Railroad Co. (the famous Vanderbilt line), the company's name was changed to Pennsylvania New York Central Transportation Co. on 1 February 1968. Three months later, it became the Penn Central Transportation Co. (8 May 1968). The Penn Central Co. was incorporated in 1969 as a holding company controlling all the outstanding stock of the transportation company. In 1970, facing bankruptcy, the subsidiary company was placed in the hands of a trustee who developed a plan of reorganisation aiming at selling all the assets unconnected with the transport business to aid recovery. Three changes were required: rationalisation of the plant, removal of unnecessary labour costs and compensation for the losses in passenger services. The Penn Central traditionaliy operated a very important commuter service in New York, Philadelphia and Boston. From the time the company started the bankruptcy proceedings, it halted payments of leases to 37 railway companies, some of which in turn went into difficulties. Because of the lack of liquidity, the Penn Central was forced in 1973 to make drastic cuts to its services, as the only railway lines with an adequate return were the New Haven Railroad and the Hudson & Harlem Railroad. After the company's liquidation in 1976, a plan of rearrangement was accepted by the majority of shareholders in July 1977. According to this, the company received approximately 10 per cent of the stock of the reorganised transportation company. This marked the end of the venerable Penn Central, a giant in the transport world, with its extensive railway network, substantial interests in pipeline operations and large-scale property developments—since the merger it owned in particular the old Vanderbilt Grand Central terminal in New York.

The Pennsylvania Slatington and New England Railroad Co.

First mortgage six per cent 30 year bearer bond for $1000 issued on 1 July 1882 by The Pennsylvania, Slatington & New England Railroad Co. This certificate formed part of a series of 1200 bonds in the same denomination. It was printed by the American Banknote Co.

The company, incorporated on 22 June 1882 as a consolidation of two railway companies, planned the construction of a line from Harrisburg (Pennsylvania) to Poughkeepsie (New York). In 1887 these bonds were partly repaid out of the proceeds of the foreclosure sale to liquidate the company as decreed by the U.S. Circuit Court in 1886.

The People's Passenger Railway Co.

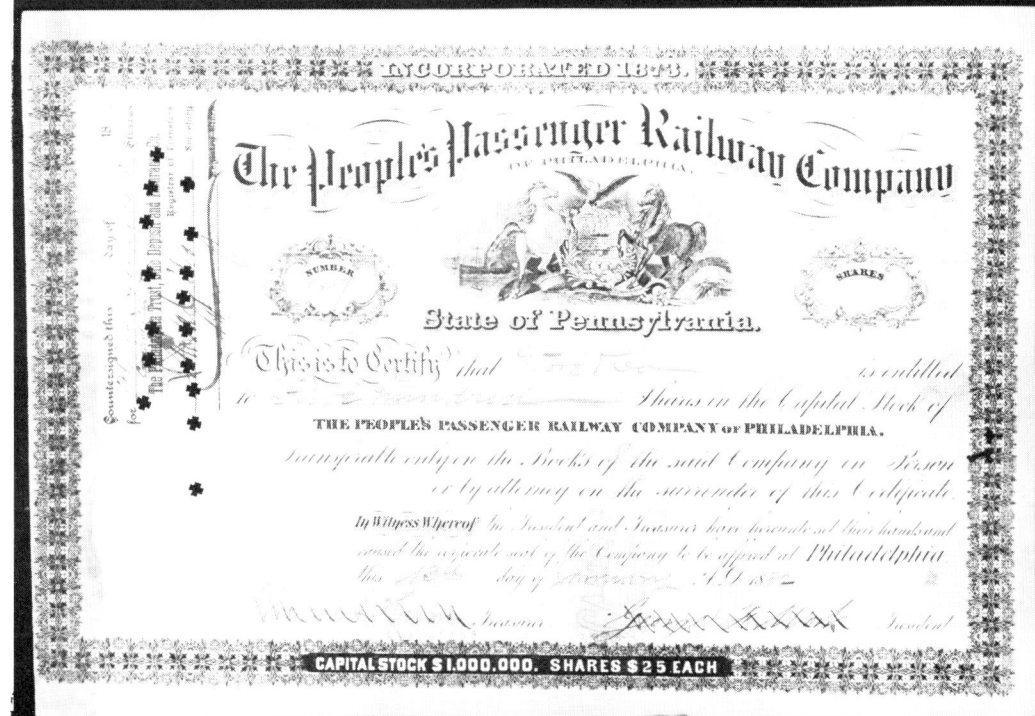

Registered certificate for 500 shares of $25 each in the People's Passenger Railway Co. of Philadelphia, dated 13 January 1882.

Chartered on 15 April 1873 to build and run a city tramway in Philadelphia, the company owned a line of approximately 3 miles in length, and used horse-drawn vehicles. The tramway was opened in 1875. From 1881, the company also leased the Germantown Passenger Railway Co. for 999 years.

Peoria & Bureau Valley Railroad Co.

Registered certificate for nine shares of $100 each in the Peoria & Bureau Valley Railroad, dated 10 August 1857. This early certificate, with an interesting vignette of a group of Red Indians armed with bows and arrows and guarding a woman and child while a steam train is seen travelling in the distance, was printed by Danforth, Wright & Co., New York and Philadelphia (a precursor to the American Banknote Co.).

From 14 April 1854 the company was leased in perpetuity to the Chicago, Rock Island and Pacific Railroad which undertook to pay all repairs, operating expenses and taxes at an annual rental of $125,000—representing eight per cent of the share capital.

The Peoria & Eastern Railway Co.

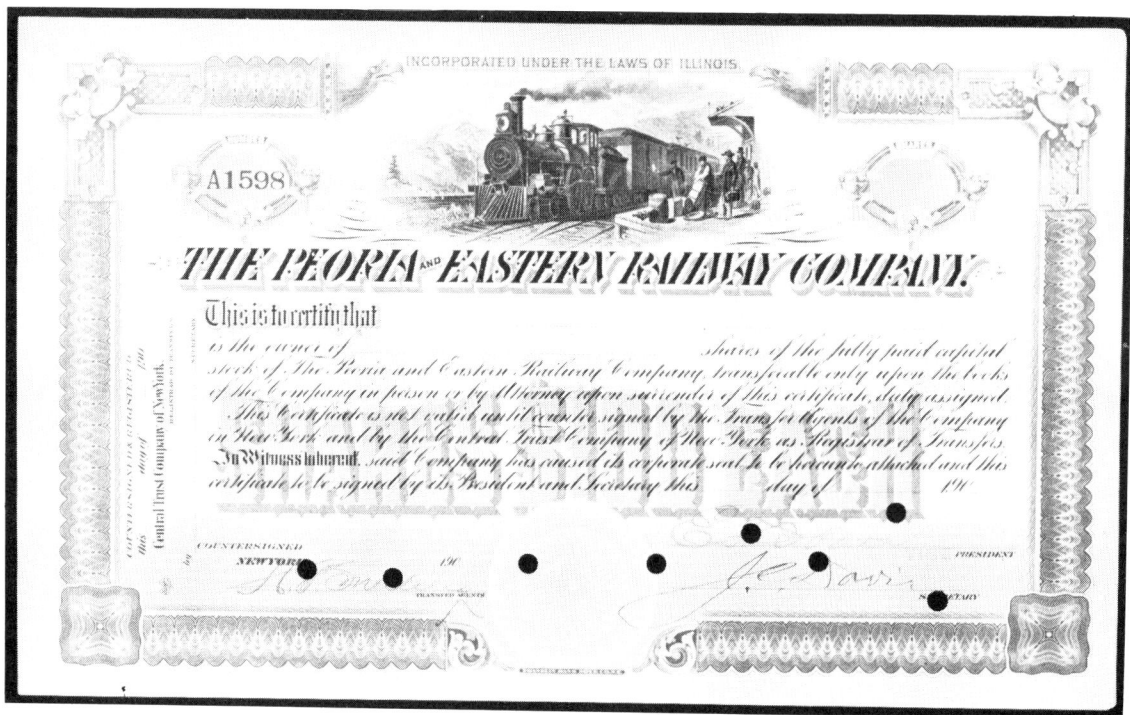

Unissued share certificate of The Peoria & Eastern Railway Co. It was printed by the Franklin Banknote Co., New York, for use during the 1900s.

The Peoria & Eastern, incorporated in Illinois, was wound up in 1940 following bankruptcy. Holders of the company's first mortgage bonds were paid 45 per cent of the face value of their bonds.

The Philadelphia & Reading Railroad Co.

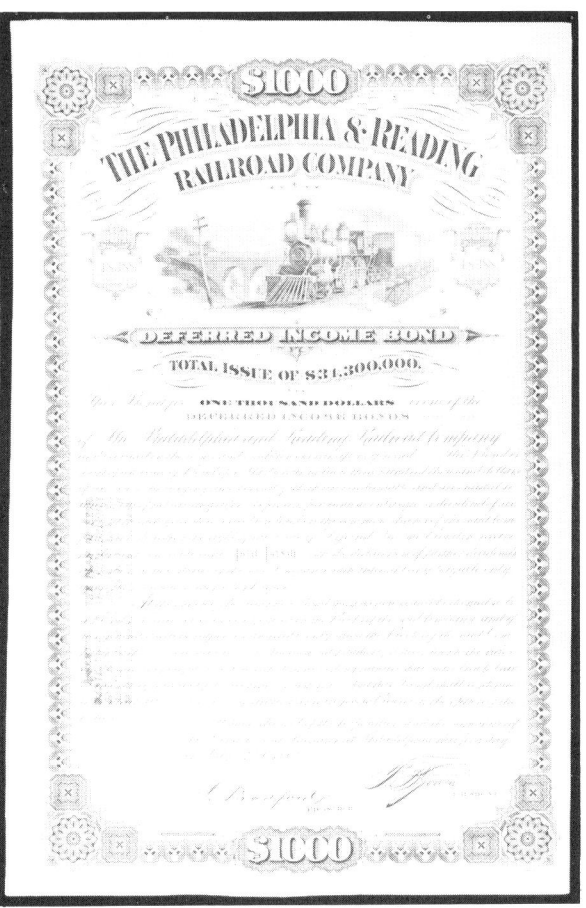

Issued on 1 July 1882 by The Philadelphia & Reading Railroad Co., this six per cent deferred income bond to bearer for $1000 formed part of a total issue of $34,300,000. Signed by Franklin B. Gowen, the company's President, the certificate was printed by the American Banknote Co. in Philadelphia.

Charted in 1833, the company opened the first section of line in 1835. Over the next few decades it extended its field of operations by several acquisitions, mergers and leases. Other than its railway network, it also leased two canal companies together with canal freight lines. The company's main business was the transport of coal from southern Pennsylvania's major anthracite coalfields to its terminus at Port Richmond, on the Delaware River, where the coal wagons could be tipped straight into vessels moored at any of the 23 wharves owned by the company. In addition, it also had a controlling interest in the Philadelphia & Reading Iron & Coal Co. As a result of the panic of 1873, the company defaulted on the payment of its maturing obligations and in 1880 had to be placed in the hands of a receiver until 1883, when its assets were returned.

Philadelphia and Western Railway Co.

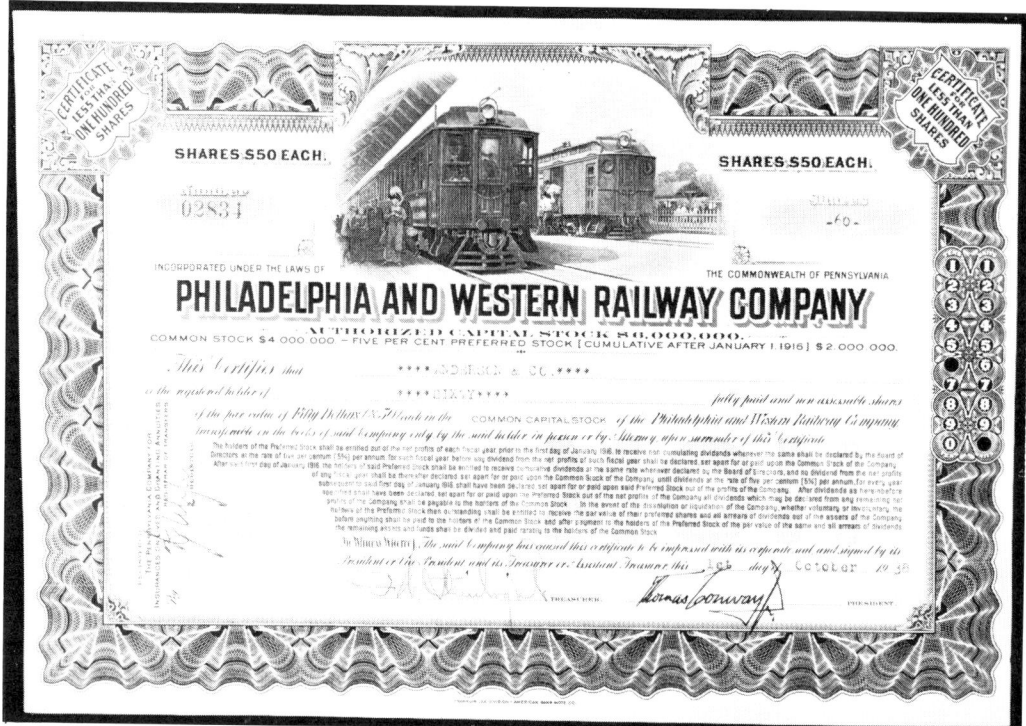

Registered certificate for 60 shares of $50 each in the Philadelphia and Western Railway Co. dated 10 October 1938. The certificate was printed by the Franklin Lee division of the American Banknote Co.

The company was incorporated in Pennsylvania in 1907, with a share capital of $6 million comprised of $4 million common and $2 million preferred shares. In 1946 it was reorganized as the Philadelphia & Western Railroad Co. which merged into the Philadelphia & Western Street Railway Co. in 1952. This company in turn was absorbed by the Philadelphia Suburban Transportation Co., which changed its name to Bryn Mawr Group, Inc. in 1970, finally becoming Bryn Mawr Camp Resorts, Inc. in 1973.

Philadelphia City Passenger Railway Co.

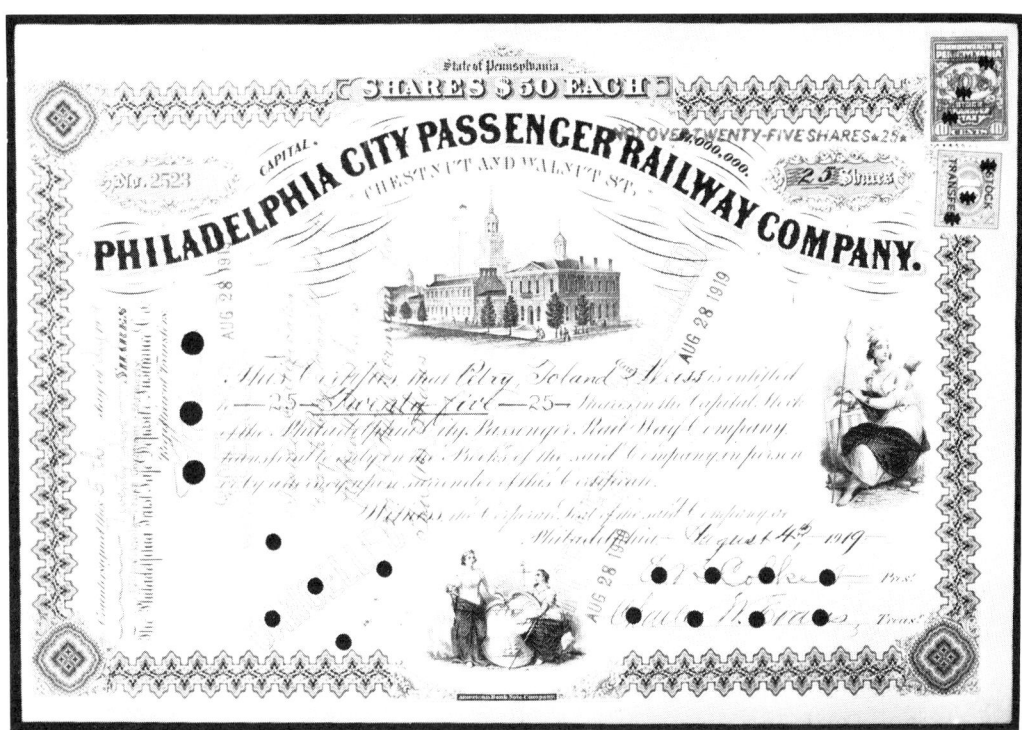

Registered certificate for 25 shares of $50 each in the Philadelphia City Passenger Railway Co., dated 4 August 1919. The certificate was printed by the American Banknote Co.

The company, which had a share capital of $1 million, had been chartered in Philadelphia in March 1859 to operate a tramway which first opened in October 1859. In 1884 it was leased for 900 years to the West Philadelphia Railroad, a rival tramway company.

Philadelphia Rapid Transit Co.

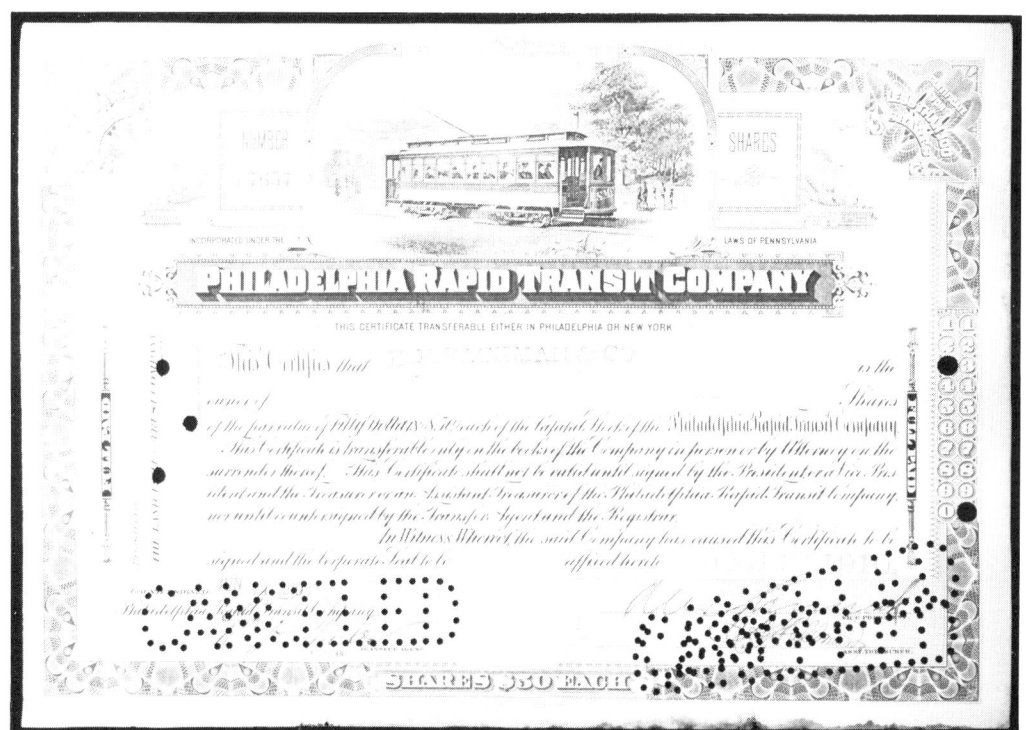

Registered certificate for 10 shares of $50 each in the Philadelphia Rapid Transit Co., dated 13 June 1910. Printed by the American Banknote Co., the certificate shows an engraving of an electric tramway, one of the company's modes of transportation.

Incorporated in Pennsylvania in May 1902, the company operated a city and suburban transport system using buses, trams and trains. In January 1940 the company was taken over by the Philadelphia Transportation Co. whose corporate existence was terminated in 1969, the final liquidation being completed in 1973.

Philadelphia Rapid Transit Co.

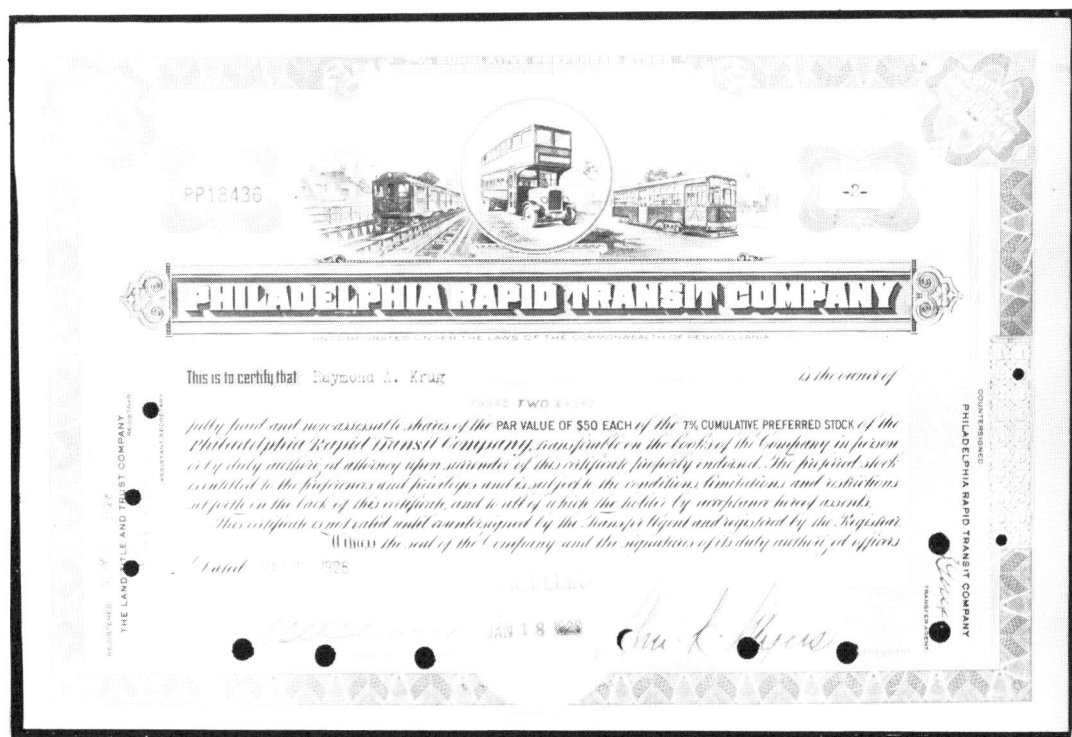

Registered certificate for two shares of $50 each of the seven per cent cumulative preferred stock of the Philadelphia Rapid Transit Co., dated 3 May 1926. The vignette on this more recent certificate was printed by the Security Banknote Co. of Philadelphia and illustrates the company's diversified means of transport.

Philadelphia Traction Co.

Registered certificate for 100 shares of $50 each in the Philadelphia Traction Co., dated 27 February 1886. The vignette on the certificate, printed by the American Banknote Co., is identical to that appearing on the certificate of the Consolidated Railway Co. of Connecticut.

The company, which operated a city and suburban tramway, was incorporated in August 1883 with a capital of $5 million. In 1886 it employed 3084 horses and 594 coaches on a network of 116 miles in length.

Philadelphia Traction Co.

Registered certificate for 100 shares of $50 each issued by the Philadelphia Traction Co. on 10 January 1908. On this later example the share capital had increased to $20 million. The vignette shows an electric tramway next to a horse-carriage. The same vignette appears on the certificates of the Omaha and Council Bluffs Street Railway Co. and the Utica and Mohawk Valley Railway Co., all three engraved by the American Banknote Co.

The Pittsburg, Shawmut and Northern Railroad Co.

First mortgage four per cent 50 year gold bond (series A) to bearer for $1000 issued on 1 February 1902 by The Pittsburg, Shawmut & Northern Railroad Co. The certificate was printed by the American Banknote Co., New York.

Incorporated in 1899 in the states of Pennsylvania and New York, the company was engaged in the transport of coal from the Pennsylvanian collieries to the major industrial centres.

Plymouth, Kankakee and Pacific Railroad Co.

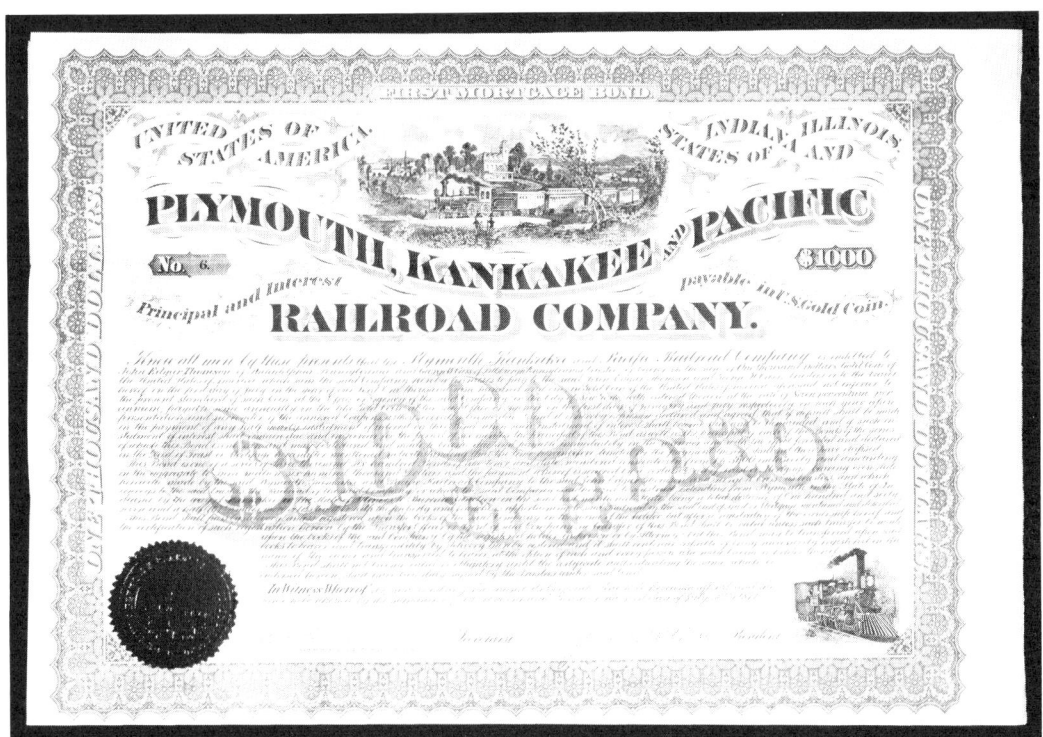

First mortgage 30 year seven per cent gold bond to bearer for $1000 issued on 1 July 1871 by the Plymouth, Kankakee and Pacific Railroad Co. It formed part of an issue of 3600 bonds of $1000 to finance the cost of constructing a railway from Plymouth, in Indiana, to Bureau Junction, via Kankakee, in Illinois, over a distance of 168 miles.

The company was incorporated in October 1870 as a consolidation of two railway companies, the Kankakee & Illinois River and the Plymouth, Kankakee & Pacific Railroad.

(This certificate is illustrated in colour—Plate 7.)

The Rio Grande Southern Railroad Co.

Unissued 50 year first mortgage five per cent gold bond to bearer for $1000 of The Rio Grande Southern Railroad Co., incorporated in Colorado. This bond formed part of a loan dated 1 July 1890 in which a series of 5000 bonds of the same denomination were issued. The certificate was printed by the Homer Lee Banknote Co., New York.

Rock Island Co.

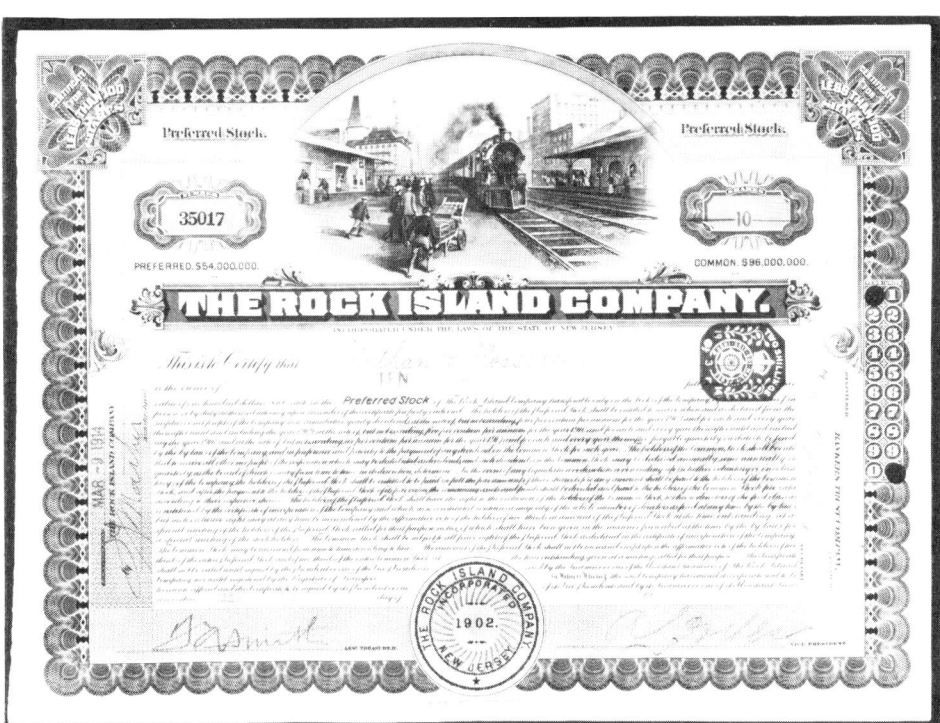

Registered certificate for 10 shares of $100 in the preferred stock of the Rock Island Co., dated 9 March 1914. On the detailed vignette of this certificate engraved by the American Banknote Co., New York, a porter pushes a baggage cart well laden with suitcases, trunks and golf bag along the platform while waiting travellers step forward to meet the train entering the station.

Incorporated in New Jersey in 1902 as a holding company with a capital of $54 million preferred and $96 million common shares, the Rock Island Co. controlled $145 million of the share capital of the Chicago, Rock Island & Pacific Railroad Co. which in turn owned the majority of shares in the Chicago, Rock Island & Pacific Railway Co. The latter emerged in 1880 as a consolidation of several railways from an original charter dating back to February 1851. The line opened from Chicago to the Mississipi River in 1854. In 1902 the Chicago, Rock Island & Pacific Railroad Co. issued $75 million of four per cent bonds secured by an identical amount of shares in the Chicago, Rock Island & Pacific Railway Co. Due to the latter's inability to pay dividends, the Railroad Company defaulted on the interest payment of its four per cent bonds. As a result, its pledge stock in the Railway Company was sold under foreclosure for $7,135,350 in 1914 to protect the bondholders who received the proceeds of the sale. This left the Rock Island Co. bereft of practically all its assets so that on 10 April 1916 it was dissolved by court order.

St. Lawrence and Adirondack Railway Co.

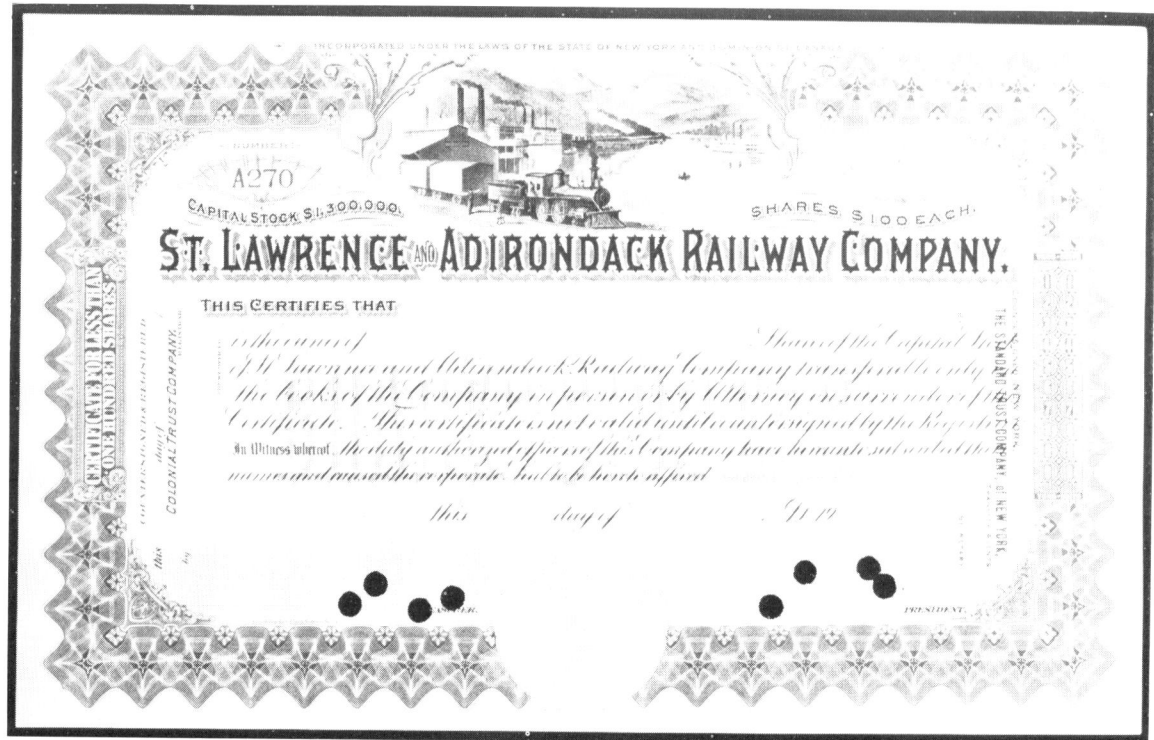

Unissued share certificate of the St. Lawrence and Adirondack Railway Co. for use in the 1900s. The certificate was printed by the Franklin Lee Banknote Co..

Incorporated in the state of New York and in Canada with a share capital of $1,300,000, the company was formerly called the Malone & Saint Lawrence Railway. It was consolidated under the existing name in November 1895, owning at that time some 12 miles of track.

State of Missouri: Saint Louis & Iron Mountain Railroad. State Bond.

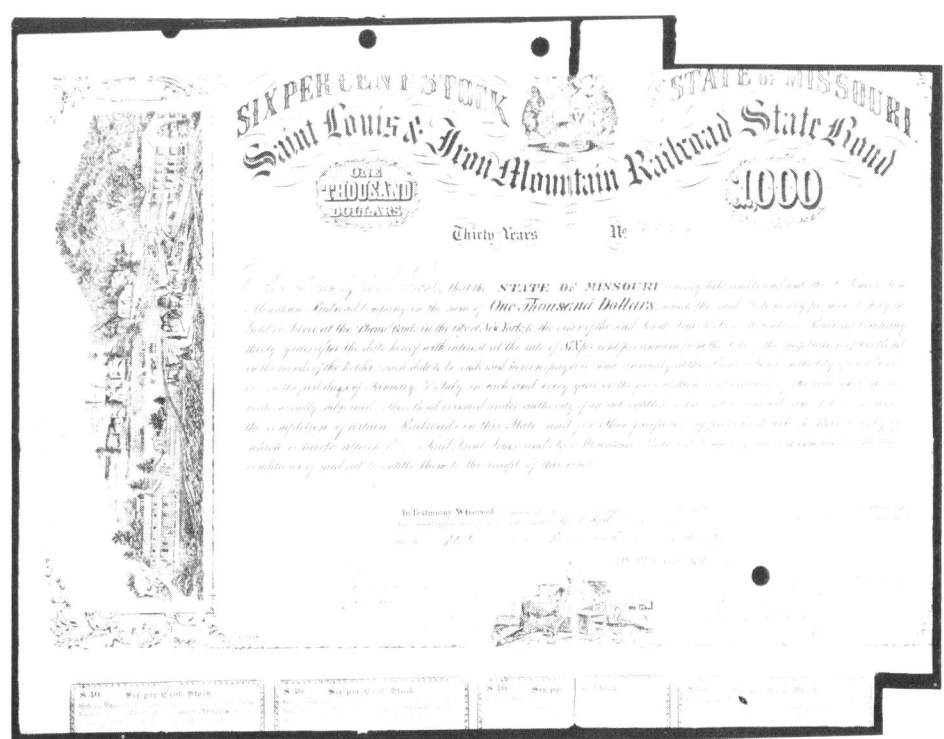

Thirty year, six per cent state bond to bearer for $1000, signed by the Governor, and issued on 11 December 1857 by the state of Missouri to finance the completion of the Saint Louis & Iron Mountain Railroad.

The 'Act to amend an Act to secure the completion of certain Railroads in this state and for other purposes', approved on 3 March 1857, provided for a credit of $740,000 to be granted to the Saint Louis & Iron Mountain Railroad Co. which received a first payment of $140,000 to be applied to the construction of the railway 'north of the Pilot Knob' in county St. Francois (Missouri). The remainder was to be divided into three instalments of $200,000 payable upon the proof that the previous sum had been expended on the actual railway construction. An additional sum of $600,000 was to be made available to the company, also against proof that half the sum granted had been spent on the railway's construction and equipment. In order to press ahead with the construction of railways in the state, the legislature of the state of Missouri authorized the issue of various state bonds in aid of several railway companies such as the Hannibal & St. Joseph, the St. Louis & Iron Mountain, the Cairo & Fulton (later merged with the St. Louis & Iron Mountain), the Southwest Branch of the Pacific Railroad. The financial crisis of 1857 brought railway development to a halt and further issues of bonds were suspended until 1859. In the government reorganisation which took place after the Civil War, a 'funding act' to liquidate the state's existing debt was passed. This provided for the funding of the debt with interest to 1868. The interest coupons of the St. Louis & Iron Mountain Railroad were paid until the end of 1868.

Saint Paul Eastern Grand Trunk Railway Co.

Unissued share certificate of the Saint Paul Eastern Grand Trunk Railway Co. for use in the 1880s. Engraved by the American Banknote Co. (New York), the vignette on this certificate illustrates one of the region's major economic activities, the lumber trade. In this instance, felled logs are seen floating down-river to the sawmill.

This company was formed in Wisconsin in September 1879 with a capital of $6 million to construct a railway from Oconto (Wisconsin) to St Paul (Minnesota). Construction began in 1882, with the state of Wisconsin making 200,000 acres of land available to the railway company on completion of the first 70 miles of track. In 1884, when 56 miles of line were completed and opened, the Milwaukee, Lake Shore & Western Railway Co. acquired control of the company, operating it through a lease. Samuel S. Sands figured among the directors elected to the board in 1885.

Second & Third Street Passenger Railway Co.

Registered certificate for one share of $50 issued on 15 July 1872 by the Second & Third Street Passenger Railway Co.

Incorporated on 10 April 1858, this company owned 37 miles of line in Philadelphia, on which it ran a horse-drawn tramway service. By the mid-1870s the company carried more than eight million passengers in one year, using 600 horses and 115 carriages and was able to declare 11 per cent dividends in 1875. It survived until 1940 when it was acquired by the Philadelphia Transportation Co., a corporation liquidated in 1968.

Southern Pennsylvania Iron and Rail Road Co.

Second mortgage 10 year seven per cent gold bond to bearer for $1000 issued on 1 September 1870 by the Southern Pennsylvania Iron and Rail Road Co. This bond formed part of a loan totalling $200,000 which was secured by a second mortgage on the railway's property and franchises.

This railway, which opened the way to valuable iron mines and furnaces, was leased by the Cumberland Valley Railroad.

South Mountain Railroad Co.

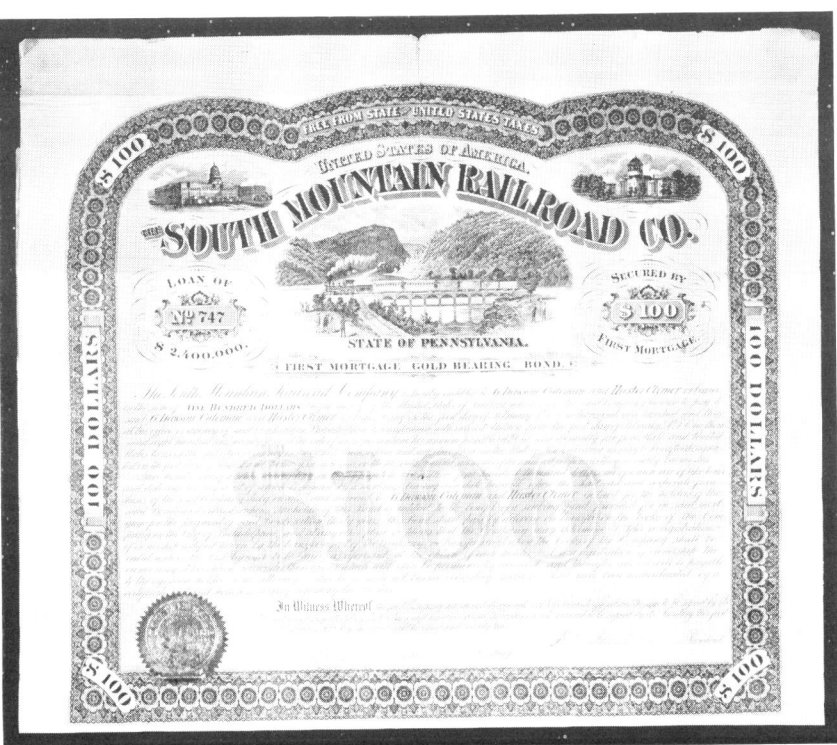

First mortgage seven per cent gold bearing bond for $100, redeemable in 1903, issued by the South Mountain Railroad Co. on 1 February 1873. This bond, signed by William H. Bell, President, and Jacob C. Heilman, Secretary, formed part of a loan of $2·4 million.

Chartered in Pennsylvania, the company commenced work on the railway in October 1872. The projected line was to extend from Harrisburg to Hamburg (Pennsylvania), over a distance of 55 miles. In the ensuing years the railway lost its separate identity and by 1882 it became part of the Pennsylvania, Slatington & New England Railroad, a company created by the consolidation of several railways.

(This certificate is illustrated in colour—Plate 8).

The South Western Rail Road Co.

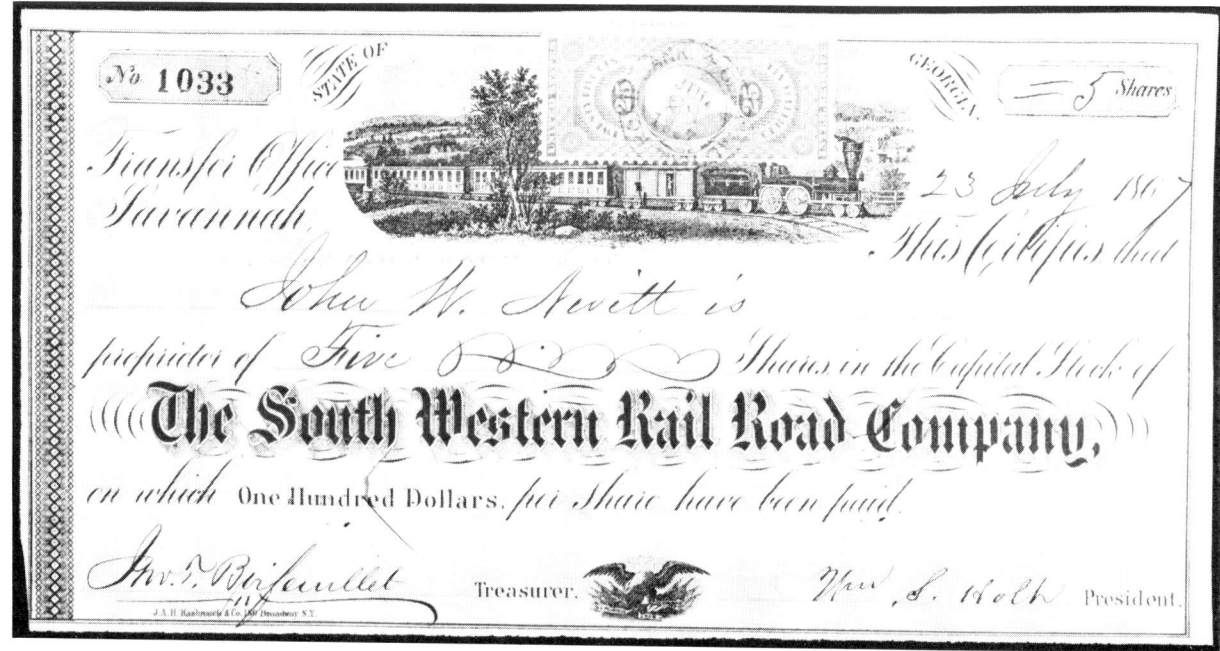

The size of a banknote, this registered certificate for five shares in the capital stock of The South Western Rail Road Co., on which $100 per share was paid, was issued on 23 July 1867. The certificate was printed by J. A. H. Hasbrouck & Co., New York.

The company, whose President at that time was William S. Holt, had been chartered in Georgia in 1845. First opened in August 1851, its line ran from Macon (Georgia) to Eufala (Alabama) over a distance of 144 miles. In addition there were a number of branch lines. In 1868 the South Western Railroad was consolidated with the Muscogee Railroad and was leased in the following year by the Central Railroad (and Banking Company) of Georgia.

The South Western Rail Road Co.

This registered certificate for 40 shares, with $100 per share paid, was issued by The South Western Rail Road Co. of Georgia on 22 May 1886. Differing from the previous example, the vignette on this certificate, lithographed by the American Banknote Co. (Philadelphia), depicts a steam train crossing a bridge.

Since the consolidation in 1868 of the South Western Railroad with the Muscogee Railroad, the length of all lines operated totalled 320 miles. From 1869, the company had been leased to the Central Railroad & Banking Co. of Georgia, the latter assuming all liabilities and agreeing to pay a minimum of seven per cent on the share capital which stood at $5,099,000 by 1886.

Syracuse & Utica Rail Road Co.

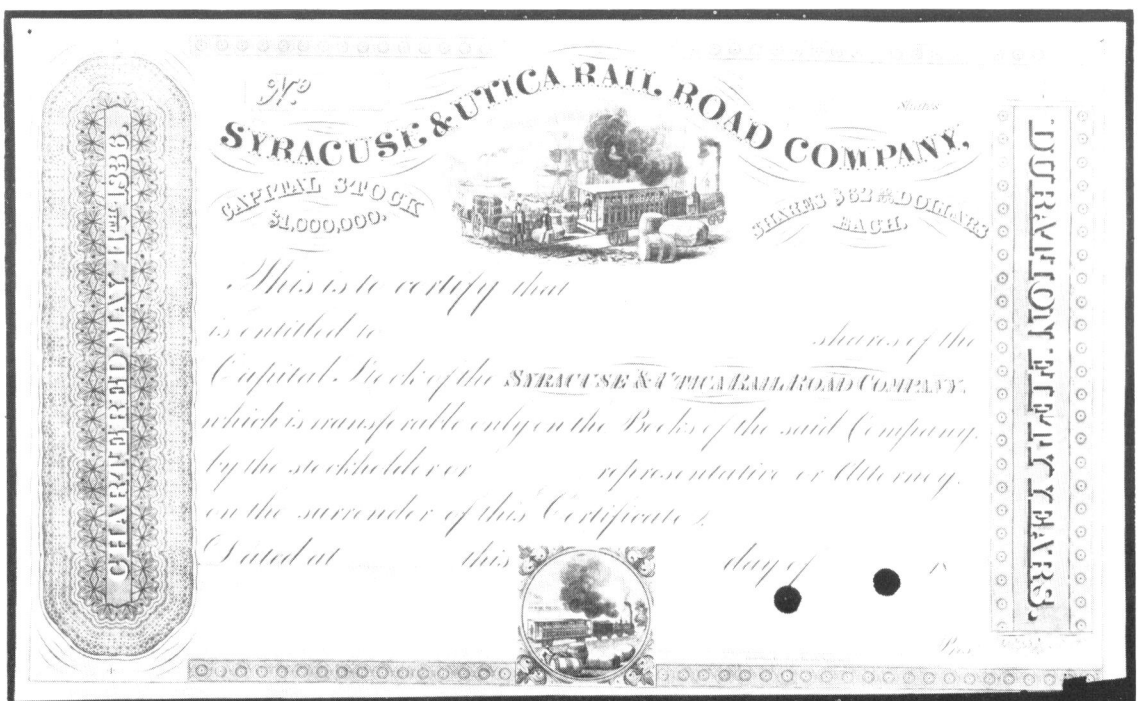

Unissued share certificate of the Syracuse & Utica Rail Road Co., which was chartered in New York on 11 May 1836 with a capital of $1 million divided unusually into shares of 62\frac{50}{100}$. The certificate was printed by Rawdon, Wright & Hatch, New York.

The Syracuse & Utica Rail Road opened for business on 3 July 1839. It lost its separate identity in 1853 after the promulgation of a special law which authorized the consolidation of several railway companies operating between Albany and Buffalo into one large corporate entity, the New York Central Railroad Co. The first board of directors of the newly-organized company was elected on 6 July 1853, and on 1 August 1853 the whole line became the property of the New York Central Railroad. In 1869 it merged with the Hudson River Railroad Co. and was acquired by Cornelius Vanderbilt.

Town of Richland: Syracuse Northern Railroad. Municipal Bond

Seven per cent bearer bond for $100 for redemption in 1890 issued on 1 March 1870 by the town of Richland, County Oswego, in the state of New York, to help in financing the construction of the Syracuse Northern Railroad. The certificate was printed by Henry Seibert & Bros., New York.

After the formation of the company on 25 February 1868 the legislature of the state of New York passed an act on 4 May 1868 "to authorize certain Towns in the counties of Onondaga, Oswego and Jefferson to issue Bonds in aid of the Syracuse Northern Railroad Company". The railway, which ran from Syracuse to Sandy Creek Junction, a distance of 45 miles, was opened during 1871–1872. In 1875, in a sale under foreclosure, the company was transferred to the Rome, Watertown & Ogdensburg Railroad Co. which operated it from then on as its Syracuse division. The bonds issued by the town of Richland were fully redeemed at the Pulaski National Bank in 1890.

Toledo, St. Louis and Western Railroad Co.

Registered prior lien 3½ per cent gold bond for $5000 issued on 1 July 1900 by the Toledo, St. Louis & Western Railroad Co., for redemption in 1925. This bond formed part of a total issue of $9 million secured by a mortgage on the company's assets, with an additional $1 million available after 1902. The certificate was printed by the Franklin-Lee Banknote Co., New York.

Incorporated in the state of Indiana in 1900, the company was consolidated in June 1923 with the New York, Chicago & Saint Louis Railroad which, after several changes in its capital structure, in turn merged into the Norfolk & Western Railway Co. in 1964.

Trenton Street Railway Co.

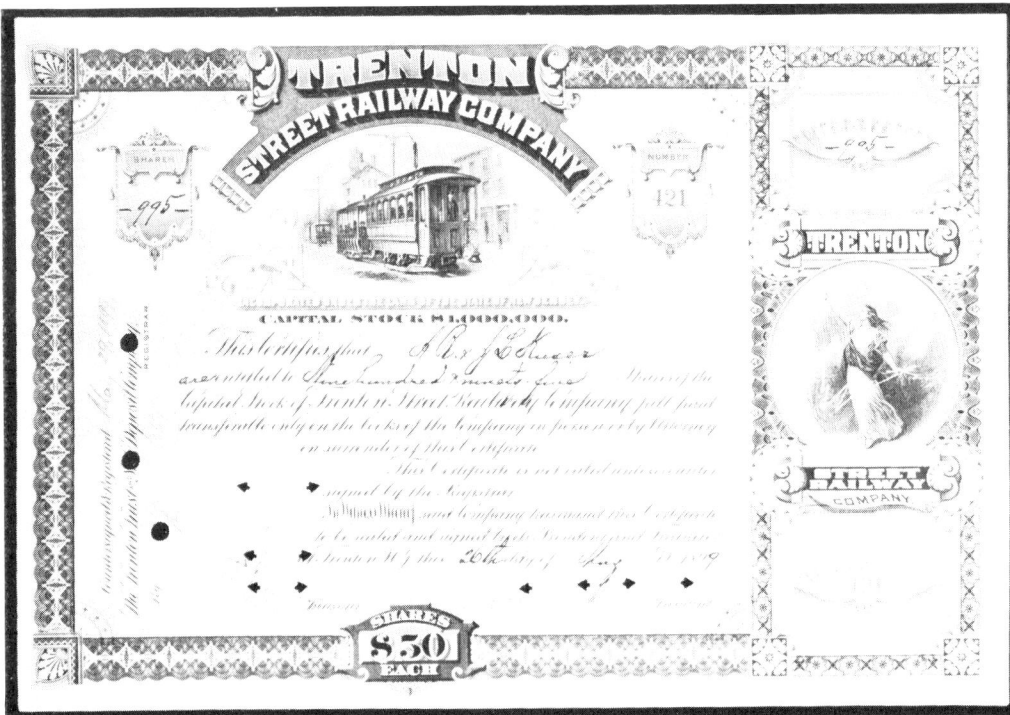

Registered certificate for 995 shares of $50 each issued on 20 May 1899 by the Trenton Street Railway Co. The certificate, with its vignettes of an electric tramway and an allegorical figure representing electricity, was engraved by the American Banknote Co., Philadelphia. The same design appears also on the Louisville Railway Co. certificates of 1893.

This corporation was formed under this name in New Jersey on 29 June 1898 by the consolidation of several tramways in Trenton.

Union Passenger Railway Co.

Registered certificate for 100 shares of $50 each in the Union Passenger Railway Co. of Philadelphia, dated 15 December 1890.

The company had been incorporated in Philadelphia to operate an originally horse-drawn tramway of 70 miles in total length, as the fine vignettes lithographed by the American Banknote Co. suggest. By 1890 the company's share capital stood at $1 million. In 1940 it was acquired by the Philadelphia Transportation Co., itself wound up in 1968.

Utica and Mohawk Valley Railway Co.

Unissued share certificate of the Utica and Mohawk Valley Railway Co. The vignette on this certificate, engraved by the American Banknote Co., New York, is also reproduced on the certificates of the Philadelphia Traction Co. and the Omaha & Council Bluffs Street Railroad Co.

Chartered by the state of New York in 1874, this company operated a horse-drawn tramway, which was later converted to electrical traction.

Vicksburg, Shreveport & Pacific Railroad Co.

Unissued share certificates of the Vicksburg, Shreveport & Pacific Railroad Co.

The railway's charter was granted in 1853 when the Vicksburg, Shreveport & Texas Railroad Co. started constructing the line which first opened in 1861 from Delta (opposite Vicksburg) to Monroe, in Louisiana, and was extended through to Shreveport in 1884. In 1862, the company leased the still uncompleted section (from Shreveport, Louisiana, to the Texan border) to the Texas & Pacific Railway Co. which took charge of its operation. Sold under foreclosure on 1 December 1879, the railway was reorganised on 2 December 1879 under the present title of Vicksburg, Shreveport & Pacific Railroad. Two years later, in the early part of 1881, it passed under the control of the Alabama, New Orleans, Texas & Pacific Junction Railways Co. Ltd., of London, a company which owned a controlling interest in several railway companies operating in the southern United States.

Wabash Railroad Co.

Registered certificate for 10 shares of $100 each in the preferred capital stock of the Wabash Railroad Co., dated 7 March 1910.

The oldest portion of the Wabash system, a line of 55 miles in length known as the Northern Cross, was chartered in 1837 to run from Quincy on the Mississippi River to the Indiana state line. The Wabash Railroad Co. emerged in 1889 as a consolidation of the Wabash Western and the Wabash, St Louis & Pacific Railway, the latter organised in 1879 and acquired between 1879 and 1880 by Jay Gould who placed some of his closest associates such as Sidney Dillon, Samuel Sloan and his son George J. Gould on the board of directors. Operating in a rich grain-producing area, the railway's chief traffic consisted in shipping grain to the Great Lakes. The strategic position of the Wabash, reflected in its advertising slogan in the late 1870s "The only central route to the West", had been well recognized by Gould who took advantage of the company's depressed share price to purchase a majority holding. Falling victim of its own severe rate-cutting policy, the Wabash, St. Louis & Pacific gradually disintegrated and was placed in the hands of a receiver. After a sale under foreclosure, a new company was organized in 1889 under the name of The Wabash Railroad Co. with Gould still holding a controlling interest. In 1915 a new Wabash Railway Co. was incorporated as successor to the Wabash Railroad which had been sold under foreclosure in July of the same year. The new company operated until 1942 when it was reorganized as the Wabash Railroad Co. This corporation passed under the control of the Norfolk & Western Railway Co. in 1970.

Waterloo, Cedar Falls & Northern Railroad

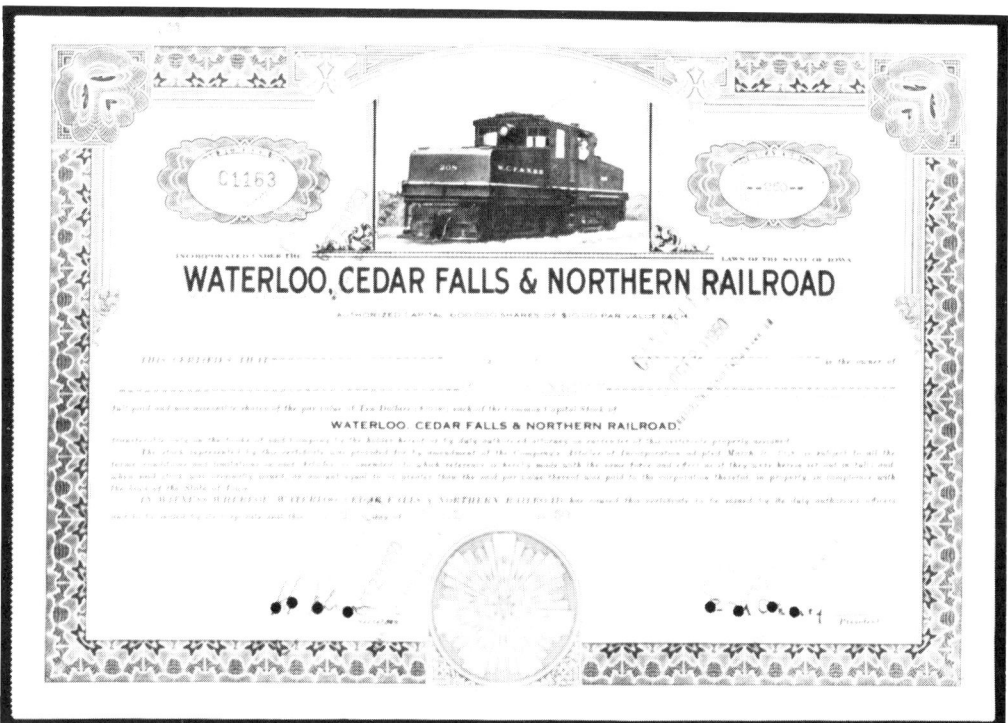

Registered certificate for 260 shares of $10 each in the common capital stock of the Waterloo, Cedar Falls & Northern Railroad, dated 18 April 1950.

This company was incorporated in Iowa in 1944 with a share capital of $6 million as successor to the Waterloo, Cedar Falls & Northern Railway Co.

Western Maryland Railroad Co.

Six per cent bond to bearer for $500, maturing on 1 January 1890, issued by the Western Maryland Railroad Co. on 30 September 1867. Bearing serial number 5, this bond formed part of a loan of $300,000 which was secured by a second mortgage on the railway's assets and endorsed by the city of Baltimore in the person of its mayor.

The company was originally chartered as the Baltimore, Carroll & Frederick Railroad Co. on 27 May 1852 but adopted the existing name in 1853. Construction of the railway from Baltimore to Williamsport, a distance of 90 miles, began in 1857. The line was completed in 1873. To help in financing the construction of the railway, the Western Maryland launched several bond issues between 1860 and 1872 to a total of $3,675,000.

Western Maryland Railroad Co.

First mortgage four per cent fifty year registered gold bond for $1000 of the Western Maryland Railroad Co. dated 31 August 1921. This bond formed part of a loan of $50 million, redeemable in 1952, which was first issued on 1 October 1902.

The company, sold under foreclosure, was reorganized as the Western Maryland Railway Co. in 1917, as a consolidation with several other Baltimore lines. It operated a railway system across Maryland, West Virginia and Pennsylvania totalling some 860 miles. As from 1930, the Baltimore & Ohio Railroad, which controlled 43 per cent of all the Western Maryland's stock, was ordered by the Interstate Commerce Commission to divest itself if its holding by turning it over to a trustee under a voting trust agreement. The latter was terminated in 1968 when control of the Western Maryland reverted to the Baltimore & Ohio Railroad which, together with the Chesapeake & Ohio Railway, held 74 per cent of the voting shares. Following the offer for the company's outstanding minority shares by the Baltimore & Ohio Railroad in 1973, the Chesapeake & Ohio and the Baltimore & Ohio Railroad companies own about 90 per cent of the Western Maryland common shares.

Western Pacific Railroad Co.

Registered certificate for two shares of $100 each of the preferred stock, series A, of the Western Pacific Railroad Co., dated 29 May 1945.

This company was incorporated under the laws of California on 6 June 1916 as a reorganisation of the Western Pacific Railway Co. which had been formed in 1903. The Western Pacific was born from a plan to build a coast-to-coast system out of Jay Gould's railways which ran chiefly from St. Louis to the Southwest. This was an ambition which he himself had never been able to fulfill before his death in 1892. In 1901 a plan was devised in which the existing Gould lines would be used as the backbone for this development. Amongst them, the Missouri Pacific was the most successful company. The acquisition of the Denver & Rio Grande carried the project as far as Ogden in Utah. Beyond this point, the Union Pacific and the Southern Pacific dominated the situation. It became necessary to build an independent line to San Francisco over the Rocky Mountains. This was the Western Pacific Railway. The cost of its construction was so great that it resulted later in a virtual collapse of the Gould system. To connect with the Atlantic coast, the Wheeling & Lake Erie had been acquired and with the take-over of the Western Maryland in 1902, only a small gap between Wheeling and Pittsburgh, over the Alleghanies, needed to be overcome. This and the cost of the Western Pacific placed such a heavy burden on the system that it could not weather through the effects of the panic of 1907 and it started to disintegrate. The Western Pacific opened in 1909 to freight service, and to passenger service in 1910, but was not financially self-sufficient. Meanwhile, the Denver & Rio Grande Railroad, which guaranteed the first mortgage bonds of the Western Pacific, failed to maintain its guarantee and was sold under foreclosure to the Western Pacific for $5 million in 1920.

In 1924 the Western Pacific Railroad Co. and the Southern Pacific Co. concluded a 50-year agreement on a joint operation of their tracks between two given points in Nevada. This gave each company the benefit of double trackage on that particular stretch of line. In 1930 the

(Continued overleaf)

Western Railroad Corporation

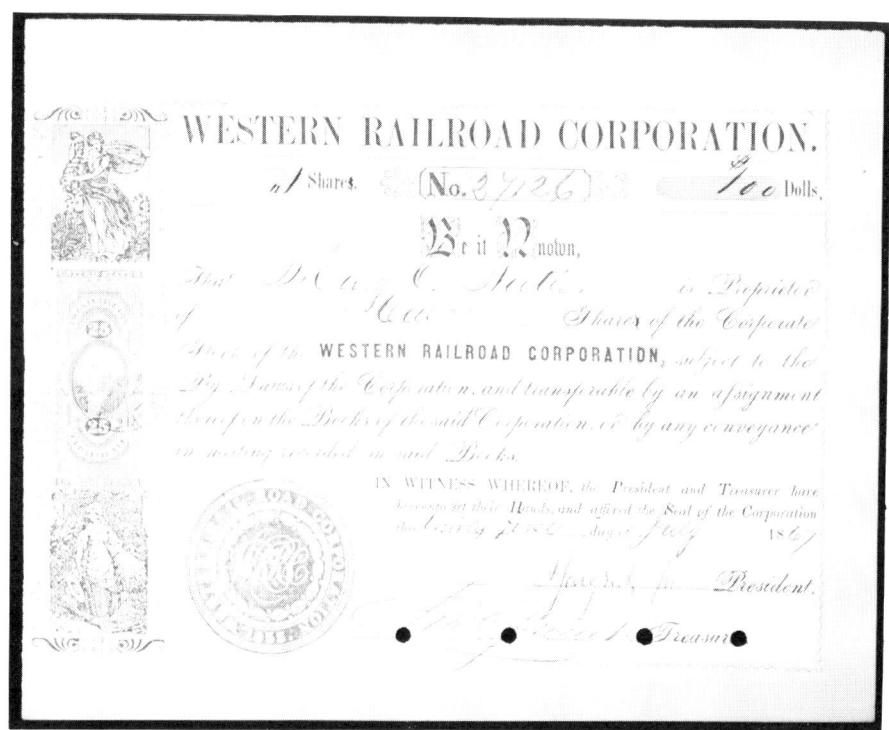

Registered certificate of one share for $100 of the Western Railroad Corporation, dated 31 July 1867. The certificate was signed by Ignatius Sargent, a director, and C. E. Stevens, the Treasurer.

Originally chartered in Massachusetts on 15 March 1833, the company merged in December 1867 with the Boston & Worcester Railroad to form the Boston & Albany Railroad, which ran 201 miles from Boston to Albany.

Western Pacific Railroad Co. *(cont. from p. 157)*

Interstate Commerce Commission granted an application by the Great Northern Railway Co. and the Western Pacific Railroad to create a new north—south route on the Pacific coast, opened in 1931, to compete with the Southern Pacific system. The portion built by the Western Pacific cost an estimated $10 million.

In 1935 the company filed a petition for reorganisation, which was eventually consummated on 29 December 1944. The share certificate illustrated here was issued under the new plan of reorganisation. On 17 June 1971, Western Pacific Industries Inc., a holding company formed in Delaware in 1970, obtained control by takeover of 96 per cent of the common stock of the Western Pacific Railroad in a share-for-share exchange. In May 1972 it acquired the remaining balance of the stock, thus making the Western Pacific Railroad a wholly-owned subsidiary of Western Pacific Industries.

Wheeling and Lake Erie Railway Co.

Registered certificate for 10 shares of $100 of the Wheeling & Lake Erie Railway Co., dated 13 December 1948. The certificate was engraved by the American Banknote Co.

This railway was first chartered in 1871 with a capital of $500,000 as the Wheeling & Lake Erie Railroad to construct a line from Wheeling, in West Virginia on the Ohio River, to Toledo (Ohio) over a distance of roughly 200 miles. Following the foreclosure sale of the Wheeling & Lake Erie Railroad Co. a reorganisation took place and the Wheeling & Lake Erie Railway was incorporated under Ohio laws on 14 December 1916. In the complicated financial history of the railway which was controlled by several companies in succession, the New York, Chicago and St. Louis Railroad purchased in 1947 the majority of the Wheeling & Lake Erie stock from the Chesapeake & Ohio Railway Co. Final control of the Wheeling & Lake Erie passed into the hands of the Norfolk & Western Railway Co. when the latter absorbed the New York, Chicago & St. Louis Railroad in 1964.

Wichita Falls and Southern Railway Co.

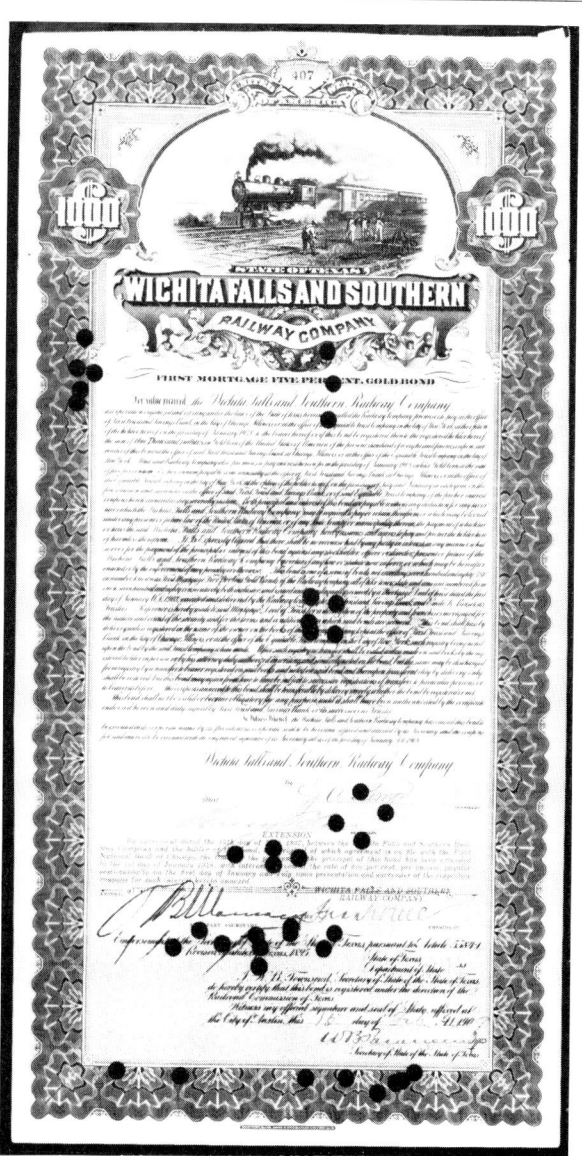

First mortgage 30-year five per cent gold bond to bearer, issued on 1 January 1908 by the Wichita Falls & Southern Railway Co.; the certificate was produced by the Western Bank Note Engraving Co, Chicago. This bond formed part of a total of 780 bonds, all in $1000 denomination, and was endorsed by the Secretary of State of the state of Texas. By an agreement reached between the company and the bondholders in 1937, the maturity of the bonds was extended until 1 January 1948. Interest on the coupons was paid until 1944 and a certain amount of the principal and interest was redeemed by the trustee, the National Bank of Chicago. The $780,000 loan raised by the company was unconditionally guaranteed by the Wichita Falls & Northwestern Railway Co. and the Wichita Falls Railway Co., both of which controlled the totality of the company's stock.

Barely two years after the loan issue, the Wichita Falls Railway Co. merged into the Wichita Falls & Northwestern. In 1911, the Missouri, Kansas & Texas Railway Co., acquired control of the latter by purchasing the majority of its shares. From then onwards, the destiny of the Wichita Falls & Northwestern (and by extension, of the Wichita Falls & Southern), was closely linked to the fate of the Missouri, Kansas & Texas Railway. When that company failed in 1915, it also brought down the Wichita Falls & Northwestern which had to be placed under receivership in 1917. In 1922 a new company, the Missouri-Kansas-Texas Railroad Co., was formed by reorganising the old Missouri, Kansas & Texas Railroad Co., and the Wichita Falls & Northwestern Railway Co.

PRICE GUIDE TO THE CERTIFICATES

Supplied by Stanley Gibbons Currency Ltd., January 1980

Arkansas Midland Railroad Co., $1000 bond, 1889	£35
Atlantic City and Shore Railroad Co., $100 share, 1906	£15
Attica and Buffalo Rail Road Co., unissued share prior to 1842	£25
Baltimore and Ohio Rail Road Co., $100 share, 1853	£50
Baltimore and Ohio Rail Road Co., 1914	£10
Baltimore and Ohio Southwestern Railway Co., $100 share, 1899	£15
Boston Consolidated Street Railway Co., 1887	£30
Boston Hartford and Erie Railroad Co., $1000 bond, 1866	£35
Boston and New York Air Line Railroad Co., $5000 bond, 1905	£25
Boston and Providence Railroad Corporation, 1871	£35
Canon City and Cripple Creek (State of Colorado) Electric Railway Co., $1000 bond, 1897	£25
Canton, Aberdeen and Nashville Rail Road Co., (State of Mississippi), $1000 bond, 1884	£18
Chicago, Burlington and Quincy Railroad Co., 1886	£10
Chicago and Eastern Illinois Railroad Co., unissued share	£12
Chicago and Eastern Illinois Railroad Co., $100 share, 1898	£15
Chicago Great Western Railroad Co., $100 share, 1937	£8
Chicago, Lake Geneva and Pacific Railway Co., unissued share	£15
Chicago and Northwestern Railway Co., $100 share, 1936	£8
Chicago, Portage and Superior Railway Co., $1000 bond, 1881	£25
Chicago, St. Paul, Minneapolis and Omaha Railway Co., $100 share, 1880	£10
Cincinnati, Indianapolis, St. Louis and Chicago Railway Co., unissued share	£8
Cincinnati, Sandusky and Cleveland Railroad Co., unissued share	£15
Cincinnati, Wabash and Michigan Railway Co., unissued share	£12
Cincinnati, Washington and Baltimore Railroad Co., unissued share	£12
Cincinnati, Washington and Baltimore Railroad Co., $100 share, 1883	£18
Citizens Passenger Railway Co. (10th and 11th Streets) Pennsylvania, $50 share, 1866	£18
Cleveland, Columbus, Cincinnati and Indianapolis Railway Co., $100 share, 1871	£18
Cleveland, Columbus, Cincinnati and Indianapolis Railway Co., $100 share, 1885	£18
Cleveland, Painsville & Ashtabula Rail Road Co., $1000 bond, 1861	£50
Cleveland, Painesville & Ashtabula Railroad Scrip, 1854	£25
(State of Ohio) Akron Branch of Cleveland and Pittsburgh Railroad Co., $1000 bond, 1852	£35
Cleveland and Toledo Rail Road Co., unissued share	£8
Colorado Midland Railway Co. (State of Colorado), $1000 bond, 1897	£18
Columbus, Springfield and Cincinnati Railroad Co., unissued share	£12
Denver and Rio Grande Railroad Co., $100 share, 1886	£15
Denver and Rio Grande Railroad Co., $100 share, 1899	£15
Denver and Rio Grande Railroad Co., 1909	£12
Detroit, Grand Rapids and Western Railroad Co., $100 share, 1899	£12
Dubuque and Sioux City Rail Road Co., $100 share, 1867	£20

Eastern and Western Air Line Railway Co., $100 share, 1886	£18
Electric Traction Co. of Philadelphia, partly paid share, 1894	£15
Erie Railroad Co., $1000 bond, 1903	£15
Escanaba, Iron Mountain and Western Rail Road Co. (State of Michigan), $1000 bond, 1890	£25
Evansville and Terre Haute Railroad Co. (State of Indiana), $1000 bond, 1880	£25
Fair Haven and Westville Railroad Co., $25 share, 1902	£15
Fitchburg and Worcester Rail Road Co., $100 bond, 1869	£18
Flint and Pere Marquette Railroad Co., $100 share, 1872	£18
Flint and Pere Marquette Railroad Co., 1883	£15
Fort Wayne and Belle Isle Railway Co., $100 share, 1892	£18
Fort Wayne, Cincinnati and Louisville Railway Co., unissued share	£12
Georgia Railroad and Banking Co., $100 share, 1842	£50
Germantown Passenger Rail Way Co., $50 share, 1894	£18
Grand Junction Rail Road and Depot Co. (Mass.), $1000 bond, 1853	£35
Grand River Valley Railroad Co., unissued share	£8
Greenville and Columbia Rail Road Co., $20 share, 1860	£25
Gulf, Mobile and Northern Railroad Co., $100 share, 1925	£4·50
Gulf, Mobile and Ohio Railroad Co., preferred stock, 1941	£3·50
Harrisburg Railways Co., $50 share, 1930	£8
Hartford and Connecticut Valley Railroad Co., $100 share, 1882	£15
Hartford and Connecticut Western Railroad Co., $100 share, 1882	£15
Hudson and Manhattan Railroad Co., unissued trust certificate	£10
Hudson and Manhattan Railroad Co., $100 share, 1947	£10
Illinois and Fox River Central Railroad Co., $500 bond, 1907	£12
Illinois Central Railroad Co., $100 share, 1919	£8
Illinois Central Railroad Co., 1954	£3
Indianapolis and Cincinnati Rail Road Co., unissued share	£15
Indianapolis, Cincinnati and Lafayette Rail Road Co., unissued share	£15
Ithaca, Auburn and Western Railway Co., $1000 bond, 1877	£30
Junction Rail Road Co., unissued share	£15
Kanawha and Michigan Railway Co., unissued share	£12
Kansas City Railways Co., $1000 bond, 1915	£18
Kansas City, St. Louis and Chicago Railroad Co., $100 share, 1914	£15
Kentucky and Great Eastern Railway Co., unissued bond	£35
Keokuk and Des Moines Railway Co., unissued share	£18
Town of Hannibal Lake Ontario Shore Railroad Co., $1000 municipal bond, 1871	£40
Lehigh Valley Railroad Co., $50 share, 1892	£18
Louisana and Missouri River Railroad Co., $100, unissued share	£18
Louisville Railway Co., $100 share, 1893	£18
Marquette, Houghton and Ontonagon Railroad Co., unissued share	£15
Michigan Central Railroad Co., unissued bond, 1902	£18
Minneapolis, St. Paul and Sault Ste. Marie Railway Co., $100 share, 1911	£15
Missouri, Kansas and Texas Railway Co., $100, 1880	£125
Missouri, Kansas and Texas Railway Co., $100, 1892	£12

Missouri, Kansas and Texas Railway Co., $100, 1895	£ 8
Missouri-Kansas-Texas Railroad Co., 1923	£ 6
Mobile and Ohio Railroad Co., $100, 1879	£18
Muscatine, Western Railway Construction Co., unissued partly paid certificate	£15
New Haven, Middletown and Williamantic Rail Road Co., unissued bond, 1870	£18
New Orleans Great Northern Railroad Co., $100 share, 1913	£ 7
New Orleans Great Northern Railway Co., $100 share, 1934	£ 7
New Orleans, Mobile and Chicago Railroad Co., 1910	£ 7
New York, Chicago and St. Louis Railroad Co., $100, 1945	£ 3·50
New York and Fort Lee Railroad Co., unissued share	£ 8
New York and Harlem Rail Road Co., $50 share, 1870	£65
New York and New England Railroad Co., $1000 bond, 1882	£35
New York and New England Railroad Co., $100 share, 1886	£18
New York and New Haven Rail Road Co., unissued bond of 1865	£35
New York, New Haven and Hartford Railroad Co., $10000 debenture, 1897	£30
New York, New Haven and Hartford Railroad Co., $10000 debenture, 1901	£30
New York, New Haven and Hartford Railroad Co., $5000 debenture, 1906	£30
New York, New Haven and Hartford Railroad Co., $10000 debenture, 1914	£30
New York, New Haven and Hartford Railroad Co., $10000 debenture, 1920	£30
New York and Northern Railway Co., unissued share	£10
New York, Ontario and Western Railway Co., $100 share, 1920	£ 8
(Town of Hastings) New York and Oswego Midland Rail Road Co., $100 bond, 1868	£35
New York, Pennsylvania and Ohio Railroad Co., $500 bond, 1880	£35
New York, Pennsylvania and Ohio Railroad Co., $50 share, 1885	£30
New York, Providence and Boston Railroad Co., partly-paid share, 1836	£50
Norfolk Southern Railroad Co., $100 share, 1936	£ 8
Old Colony and Newport Railway Co., $100 share, 1871	£20
Omaha and Council Bluffs Street Railway Co., $100 share, 1912	£12
Penn Central Co., 1975	£ 3
Pennsylvania, Slatington and New England Railroad Co., $1000 bond, 1882	£20
People's Passenger Railway Co., $25 share, 1882	£16
Peoria and Bureau Valley Railroad Co., $100 share, 1857	£28
Peoria and Eastern Railway Co., unissued share	£ 7
Philadelphia and Reading Railroad Co., $1000 bond, 1882	£25
Philadelphia and Western Railway Co., $50 share, 1938	£12
Philadelphia City Passenger Railway Co., $50 share, 1919	£12
Philadelphia Rapid Transit Co., $50 share, 1910	£12
Philadelphia Rapid Transit Co., $50, 1926	£12
Philadelphia Traction Co., $50 share, 1886	£ 8
Philadelphia Traction Co., $50 share, 1908	£ 8

Pittsburg, Shawmut and Northern Railroad Co., $1000 bond, 1902	£15
Plymouth, Kankakee and Pacific Railroad Co., $1000 bond, 1871	£35
Rio Grande Southern Railroad Co., unissued bond, 1890	£15
Rock Island Co., $100 share, 1914	£12
St. Lawrence and Adirondack Railway Co., unissued share	£10
Saint Louis and Iron Mountain Railroad, Missouri, State bond, $1000 bond, 1857	£50
Saint Paul Eastern Grand Trunk Railway Co., unissued share	£15
Second and Third Street Passenger Railway Co., $50 share, 1872	£12
Southern Pennsylvania Iron and Rail Road Co., $1000 bond, 1870	£35
South Mountain Railroad Co., $100 bond, 1873	£65
South Western Rail Road Co., 1867, share cert.	£35
South Western Rail Road Co., 1886, share cert.	£18
Syracuse and Utica Rail Road Co., unissued share	£12
(Town of Richland) Syracuse Northern Railroad, $100 municipal bond, 1870	£35
Toledo, St. Louis and Western Railroad Co., $5000 bond, 1900	£15
Trenton Street Railway Co., $50 share, 1899	£15
Union Passenger Railway Co., $50 share, 1890	£12
Utica and Mohawk Valley Railway Co., unissued share	£12
Vicksburg, Shreveport and Pacific Railroad Co., unissued share	£12
Wabash Railroad Co., $100 share, 1910	£12
Waterloo, Cedar Falls and Northern Railroad, $10 share, 1950	£4·50
Western Maryland Railroad Co., $500 bond, 1867	£35
Western Maryland Railroad Co., $1000 bond, 1921	£18
Western Pacific Railroad Co., $100 share, 1945	£3
Western Railroad Corporation, $100 share, 1867	£25
Wheeling and Lake Erie Railway Co., $100 share, 1948	£6
Wichita Falls and Southern Railway Co., $1000 bond, 1908	£18

APPENDIX

Biographies of Cornelius Vanderbilt and Jay Gould

Prior to about 1865, railway companies were mainly of local interest; a few hundred miles in length was regarded as best for efficient railway management. Only one railway exceeded 1000 miles, and as tracks were not of standard width, it was usually impossible for trains to run over the tracks of a neighbouring company. However, from the mid-1860s, the trend was for consolidation of smaller companies into large ones.

In this development which extended right through the latter half of the 19th century, vast private fortunes were accumulated by a small handful of men who seized the opportunities that presented themselves at a time when the general public was for ever demanding more and more railway construction and was in the grip of widespread railway speculation fever. Two outstanding figures dominated much of America's railway history, namely Cornelius Vanderbilt, the constructor, and Jay Gould, the manipulator. Both exploited the situation to their own profit in different ways.

Cornelius Vanderbilt (1794–1877)

Born on Staten Island on 27 May 1794, the son of a Dutch farmer who worked also as a ferryman, Cornelius Vanderbilt started his astonishing career by rowing ferry-boats across the Hudson River. He was barely in his twenties when he became the proud owner of several sailing boats. Much to everybody's surprise, he sold them all one day in 1818 to accept a salaried position as steamboat captain on the New York–New Brunswick ferry line owned by William Gibbons. Ten years later, Captain Vanderbilt went into business for himself. In 1829, he built his first steamboat. Soon, he was actively competing against other rival owners. He ended up victorious in these struggles for monopolies after disposing of his various competitors.

For over 30 years, Vanderbilt was let alone to control his fleet of some 50 boats upon the Hudson River. During the early Gold Rush in the 1850s, Vanderbilt extended the range of his activities to the Pacific Ocean to capture the California-bound traffic. With the Accessory Transit Co. providing the connecting link across Nicaragua, he ran a fleet of steamers on both oceans in direct competition with the Pacific Mail Co. which used the Isthmus of Panama. Smashing their monopoly, Vanderbilt kept his boats running until he was bought off by his rival. His last steamship was the *Vanderbilt*, which he donated to the government during the Civil War—or, as it is also alleged, which the government retained following a scandal involving Vanderbilt supply ships.

Known as 'The Commodore', Vanderbilt was nearly 70 and worth some $10 million when he sold out his shipping interests and turned to railways. In 1873, he told a reporter: 'Railroads help to develop our commerce and civilisation, and ought to be encouraged. I would like to see them stretching to every corner of the United States'. His first venture was buying Harlem Railroad stock in the early 1860s. It was selling at $8 or $9 a share, having been as low as $3. When he gained control of the company in January 1863, he applied for permission to extend the railway right into the city. This was granted in April 1863. Harlem stock, already rising, advanced to $75. At that moment, members of the city council, allied with Daniel Drew, started to sell short. The Commodore kept on buying the shares offered amid rumours that the franchise would be cancelled. Indeed, on 25 June 1863, the Board of Aldermen revoked the franchise it had granted only a few months earlier. The stock dropped, but only a few points. When the surprised short-sellers tried to close their position, there were no shares to be had and the stock rose fast, to $100, 150, 170 and $179. The dismayed council members had to settle at the highest figure. Vanderbilt raked in some $5 or $6 million. A year later, in 1864, the same trick was tried again. The Commodore's franchise was being discussed by the Legislature in Albany. He had the majority of the members on his side and the governor's promise to sign the bill. In anticipation, Harlem stock rose from $75 to $150 in the early months of 1864. But Daniel Drew and several members of the legislature came upon the idea of selling vast quantities of the stock short in advance of rejecting the bill, in a repeat performance of the former unsuccessful bear-raid. The bill was duly defeated and the shares slumped to $90. The short-sellers were so sure of ruining Vanderbilt that they had oversold the stock by some 27,000 shares. However, the Commodore, supported by friends, had bought up everything. When the 'bears' wanted to cover, they found no stock available: Vanderbilt's brokers had all the shares securely locked up in strong boxes. In his anger at being double-crossed for the second time, Vanderbilt swore he would see the stock at $1,000 before settling. But his friends pointed out that it would cause certain ruin to every single broking house in Wall Street. Relenting, he agreed to settle at $285 a share. In this transaction, Drew was reported to have lost $1 million.

Not long afterwards, Vanderbilt successfully manipulated the stock of the Hudson River Railroad, a competing line for the Harlem. The shares advanced considerably. Impressed by Vanderbilt's methods of financing, the managers of the ailing New York Central Railroad offered him the railway in 1867 almost at his own price, asking him to do for it what he had achieved with the Harlem and the Hudson River. In 1869, the Hudson River and the New York Central consolidated as the New York Central and Hudson River Railroad Co., with a capital of $90 million, while the Harlem Railroad was leased to it.

Vanderbilt acquired many more railways in subsequent years, the Canada Southern, the Michigan Central, the Lake Shore which was in debt to the tune of $7 million and managed to pay dividends within two years of his taking control. His organisational and managerial ability was considerable. The investing public was only too eager to follow him in his plans for transforming or improving a railway. His favourite method of attracting capital was by 'watering' the stock. He was always increasing the capitalisation of his railways. After gaining control of the Hudson River Railroad, he issued $7 million of new stock. He absorbed the New York Central and inflated the stock by $23 million. When the two railways consolidated, their stock increased by yet another $23 million. These operations were always kept very secret—'I never tell what I am going to do till I have done it'. Although his railways made profits and public confidence in him was high, his successes were often the result of ruthless management—for example wages were sometimes cut and economies made to achieve profitability. Tall and impressive in stature, he was imagined to be in robust and vigorous health, but at the time of his death, his doctors recorded that he had 'scarce a sound organ in his body' and that he had been a 'dyspeptic through life'. During his last six months, he was apparently hardly able to stand. 'If all the devils in hell were concentrated in me, I could not have suffered more', he told his doctor.

When he died, aged eighty-two, on 4 January 1877, Cornelius Vanderbilt left approximately $100 million. Most of his fortune was inherited by his son, William H. Vanderbilt who proceeded to treble it within seven years.

Jay Gould (1836–1892)

A quiet, devout and home-loving man whom the public called 'The Corsair' and 'The Skunk of Wall Street', Gould was born on 27 May 1836 at Roxbury, Delaware County, in the state of New York. His father was a farmer who also kept a grocery store. Gould was a sickly but studious child who constantly strove to improve his basic education. He left school at 15 to work in the village store, learning mathematics in his leisure hours in order to become a surveyor. Soon, he was employed as an assistant in a firm of surveyors engaged in preparing maps of the surrounding counties (in his spare time, he wrote a history of his home county).

A little later, in his twenties, he got into the tannery business, backed by a local financier who soon afterwards sold out to Gould because of discrepancies in the accounts. In 1863, Gould married the daughter of a wealthy merchant; the father-in-law owning some shares in a railway in bad financial condition. Having examined the railway, Gould saw its potential and took the shares for himself at the going market price, bought even more of them until he controlled the railway which he then sold out to a rival company at a profit. This was his first experience with railway transactions. He entered Wall Street, joining a firm of brokers which took the name of Smith, Gould and Martin. Gould quickly established a reputation for dealing in railways. His usual procedure was to buy up two or more financially distressed railways, consolidate them under a new name and float a large issue of bonds on the market, accompanied by publicity extolling the new company's potential. Meanwhile, he would wait for a purchaser to whom he would sell at a profit. If the purchaser failed to run the railway profitably, Gould would buy it back at greatly reduced prices and reorganise again.

During the years he served as a director on the board of the Erie Railroad, Gould was able to lay the broad foundations of his fortune. In 1867 he, together with Daniel Drew, and Jim Fisk, became directors of the Erie Railroad. Soon after Vanderbilt made unsuccessful attempts to gain control of the railroad. By various manipulations, Gould and Fisk increased their control of the Erie Railroad and in 1868 Gould became the company's president.

A new era of unbridled stock manipulation and gross mismanagement followed. In eight years, the railway's capitalisation increased by $60 million. Gould argued this was imperative to prevent Vanderbilt from grasping hold of the company. During the gold conspiracy of 1869 Gould pushed the price of gold up in an attempt to corner the gold market then, made the bubble burst at his friends' and the general public's expense in order to save himself. Public opinion turned against him, the press portraying him as evil incarnate. Taking advantage of the prevailing mood, Gould's various opponents and the long-suffering shareholders, among whom there was a great number of irate British investors, joined forces to oust him and regain control of the railway. Taken to court in 1874, Gould agreed to restore $6 million in stocks and resign from the Erie board if all pending suits against him were withdrawn.

From the money and the experience gained with the Erie Railroad, Gould went on acquiring railways until he seemed to hold the transcontinental business in his hands, controlling as he did the Union Pacific, Wabash and other western railways. Later he acquired Western Union, through which he obtained a practical monopoly on telegraphs.

He became first interested in the Pacific railways in 1873, buying 100,000 shares when the price was depressed and was made a director in 1874. In 1878, he turned his attention to the Kansas Pacific. He acquired the practically worthless Denver Pacific on speculation that it would consolidate with the Union Pacific. Amid much controversy which forced him to resign from Union Pacific Gould bought a controlling stake in Missouri Pacific for $3·8 million.

Many of Gould's schemes were ostensibly managed by one or more of his business partners, while he himself kept a low profile. By 1880, he controlled some 10,000 miles of railway, mainly in the south west of the United States. None of the Gould lines ran east of the Mississipi.

An unostentatious and reserved man, he was accused among others of betraying his friends and of inciting industrial revolt by cutting wages (he had a reputation of being tough with strikers).

When he died from T.B. in 1892, aged 56, he left his family $72 million, one of the greatest single American fortunes built in one generation. His son George J. Gould was to inherit his vast railway empire. Gould's private life could not be faulted, although his career as a financier had been marked by a series of scandals, the notorious Erie episode and his dealings in gold casting him firmly in the villain's role. Initially a speculator and a clever stock manipulator he later became more interested in railway construction. He had visions of creating a railway system which would open up the Pacific states. 'I am not interested in eastern roads', he said once, 'I am interested only in roads to the West'.

Gould's particular abilities were in corporate finance and security trading. He had a particular flair for detecting opportunities to seize control and displayed a strong sense of objectivity in appraising a situation. He showed the same lack of emotion in choosing his business associates, allying himself with former enemies if it suited, or dropping friends if they ceased being useful.